Savoring 95 Classics: A Cookbook

De Pasta Passionate

Contents

INTRODUCTION

Welcome to Savoring 93 Classics: A Cookbook! This cookbook is the ultimate guide for anyone who loves to cook and wants to explore the classics. We have taken the best of the traditional recipes passed down in family kitchens for generations and curated them into this book. From appetizers to main courses and desserts, this cookbook provides recipes for all sorts of classic dishes that your family will love.

For the culinary novice, you will find easy-to-follow recipes accompanied by clear, step-by-step instructions. For the experienced home chef, this cookbook contains recipes that will challenge and elevate your cooking skills. Either way, Savoring 93 Classics: A Cookbook is sure to become your new go-to source for recipes.

In this cookbook you will find classic dishes from all over the world, from America to Europe to Asia. You will find classic recipes for items such as French Onion Soup, Cassoulet, Shepherd's Pie, and Baked Alaska, as well as regional specialties like Hindenburg Cake (Germany) and Paul Bocuse's Fondant Potatoes (France).

In addition to offering recipes for classic dishes, this cookbook also includes interesting tidbits of history and helpful cooking tips. With its clear instructions and flavorful recipes, you'll be sure to get the most out of every dish.

From home cooks to professional chefs, Savoring 93 Classics: A Cookbook is sure to bring people of all skill levels together in the kitchen. So, grab your apron and join us on this journey of classic recipes from all over the world. Bon Appétit!

1. Classic French Onion Soup

Classic French onion soup is a comforting, flavorful soup with sweet caramelized onions and a savory, cheesy crouton topping. It's perfect dish for chilly winter days and special occasion dinners.
Serving: 8
Preparation Time: 25 minutes
Ready Time: 1 hour, 5 minutes

Ingredients:
-4 tablespoons butter
-6 large yellow onions, thinly sliced
-2 tablespoons all-purpose flour
-2 tablespoons brown sugar
-1 ½ teaspoon salt
-1/2 teaspoon ground black pepper
-2 teaspoon fresh thyme, chopped
-8-10 cups beef broth
-2 tablespoons Worcestershire sauce
-2 bay leaves
-1/2 cup dry sherry
-2 tablespoons cognac or brandy
-8 (1/2-inch-thick) slices French bread, toasted
-1 ½ cups grated Parmesan cheese

Instructions:
1. In a large pot or Dutch oven, melt butter over medium heat. Add onions and cook, stirring occasionally until caramelized, about 25 minutes.
2. Reduce heat to low and sprinkle flour over onions. Stir until flour is absorbed and cook for 3 minutes.
3. Stir in brown sugar, salt, pepper, thyme, beef broth, Worcestershire sauce, bay leaves, sherry, and cognac. Increase heat to medium-high and bring to a gentle boil.
4. Reduce heat to low, cover, and simmer for 40 minutes.
5. Preheat oven to 350 degrees F (175 degrees C). Arrange toasted bread slices in an oven safe bowl. Ladle soup into bowls over the bread. Sprinkle with Parmesan cheese.

6. Place bowls on a baking sheet. Bake for 10 minutes until cheese is melted and bubbling. Serve hot.

Nutrition information:
Calories: 193, Total Fat: 8 g, Saturated Fat: 4 g, Cholesterol: 18 mg, Sodium: 1325 mg, Carbohydrates: 23 g,protein: 7 g, Sugars: 5 g

2. Coq au Vin

Coq au Vin is a traditional French dish that consists of chicken braised in wine, lardons (bacon), mushrooms and herbs.
Serving: 4-6
Preparation Time: 30 minutes
Ready Time: 1 hour 30 minutes

Ingredients:
-3 tablespoons olive oil
-4 strips bacon, chopped
-4 chicken thighs, bone-in and skin on
-Kosher salt
-4 cloves garlic, minced
-2 cups mushrooms, roughly chopped
-1/2 cup flour
-2 cups chicken broth
-2 cups dry red wine
-1 bay leaf
-2 sprigs fresh thyme
-1 cup frozen pearl onions, thawed

Instructions:
1. Heat the olive oil in a large pot over medium heat.
2. Add the bacon and cook until lightly browned, about 3 minutes.
3. Add the chicken thighs to the pot and season them with salt.
4. Cook the chicken for about 5 minutes, or until golden brown.
5. Add the garlic and mushrooms to the pot and cook for an additional 3 minutes.
6. Sprinkle the flour over the chicken and cook for 1 minute.

7. Pour the broth, wine, bay leaf and thyme into the pot and bring to a boil.

8. Reduce the heat to low and simmer for 40-45 minutes, or until the chicken is cooked through and the sauce has thickened.

9. Add the pearl onions to the pot and simmer for an additional 10 minutes.

10. Serve the Coq au Vin with your favorite sides and enjoy!

Nutrition information: Calories: 390, Total Fat: 13g, Saturated Fat: 3g, Cholesterol: 104mg, Sodium: 375mg, Carbohydrates: 17g, Protein: 32g, Fiber: 2g

3. Beef Bourguignon

Beef Bourguignon is a classic French beef stew, made with slow-cooked chuck beef, red wine, bacon, and mushrooms. This comforting winter meal is a favorite amongst cozy family dinners and holiday feasts.

Serving: 6-8

Preparation time: 20 minutes

Ready time: 3 hours 30 minutes

Ingredients:

2 lbs chuck beef, cut into 1-inch cubes

2 tablespoons olive oil

8 oz bacon, diced

1 onion, diced

3 cloves garlic, minced

2 tablespoons all-purpose flour

3 tablespoons tomato paste

1 cup dry red wine

2-3 cups beef stock

2 carrots, diced

1 teaspoon fresh thyme

1 bay leaf

2 tablespoons butter

16 oz mushrooms, sliced

2 tablespoons chopped fresh parsley

Instructions:

1. Heat 1 tablespoon olive oil in a large Dutch oven or heavy-bottomed pot over medium-high heat. When the oil is hot, add the bacon and cook for 4-5 minutes until crisp.
2. Remove the bacon from the pot and set aside, leaving the fat in the pot.
3. Add the remaining 1 tablespoon of olive oil to the pot. When the oil is hot, add the onion and cook for 3-4 minutes until softened.
4. Add the garlic, and cook for another 30 seconds or so.
5. Add the flour and tomato paste, stirring continuously for 1-2 minutes.
6. Pour in the red wine and beef stock, and stir to combine.
7. Add the beef cubes, carrots, thyme, and bay leaf to the pot. Stir to combine.
8. Bring the mixture to a simmer, then reduce the heat to low and cover the pot. Simmer for approximately 2 ˝ hours, stirring occasionally.
9. About 30 minutes before the stew is finished cooking, heat a large skillet over medium heat. Add the butter to the skillet, then add the mushrooms and sauté until tender, about 5 minutes.
10. Add the mushrooms to the stew and cook for the remaining 30 minutes.
11. Taste the stew for seasoning and add salt and pepper, if necessary. Stir in the chopped parsley.

Nutrition information (per serving): 500 calories, 28g fat, 9g saturated fat, 33g protein, 22g carbohydrates, 4g fiber, 2g sugar, 78mg cholesterol, 688mg sodium

4. Bouillabaisse

Bouillabaisse is a traditional French Mediterranean seafood stew, brimming with succulent prawns, squid, and a medley of other fresh seafood. The unique flavors of this classic delicacy are derived from a mix of aromatic vegetables, herbs, and saffron.
Serving: Serves 6
Preparation Time: 25 minutes
Ready Time: 1 hour

Ingredients:

- 2 tablespoons extra virgin olive oil
- 1 large onion, chopped
- 2 celery stalks, chopped
- 2 garlic cloves, minced
- 2 teaspoons tomato paste
- 1 teaspoon fennel seeds
- 1 teaspoon dried oregano
- 1 teaspoon yellow mustard seed
- 1 teaspoon paprika
- ¼ teaspoon dried thyme
- 2 bay leaves
- ½ teaspoon saffron threads
- 1 teaspoon sea salt
- 6 cups vegetable broth
- 1 (14-ounce) can diced tomatoes
- ½ cup white wine
- 2 pounds firm white fish fillets, cut into cubes
- 12 jumbo raw shrimp, peeled and deveined
- 12 mussels, scrubbed and debearded
- 12 clams, scrubbed
- 2 tablespoons chopped fresh parsley
- 2 tablespoons chopped fresh basil

Instructions:
1. In a large pot or Dutch oven, heat the oil over medium heat. Add the onion, celery, garlic, tomato paste, fennel seed, oregano, mustard seed, paprika, thyme, and bay leaves. Sauté until the vegetables are softened, about 5 minutes.
2. Add the saffron, sea salt, vegetable broth, diced tomatoes, and white wine; stir to combine. Increase heat to high and bring to a boil. Reduce heat and simmer for 15 minutes.
3. Add the fish cubes, shrimp, mussels, and clams; stir to combine. Simmer until the fish and seafood are cooked through and the mussels and clams have opened, about 10 minutes.
4. Garnish with parsley and basil. Serve hot.

Nutrition information:
- Calories: 320 kcal
- Carbohydrates: 21 g
- Protein: 30 g

- Fat: 10 g
- Saturated Fat: 2 g
- Cholesterol: 143 mg
- Sodium: 1217 mg
- Potassium: 548 mg
- Fiber: 4 g
- Sugar: 7 g
- Vitamin A: 1353 IU
- Vitamin C: 30 mg
- Calcium: 164 mg
- Iron: 5 mg

5. Ratatouille

Ratatouille is a vegetable dish from Provence, France, that is known for its classic combination of flavors and textures. This healthy and flavorful dish features eggplants, zucchini, onions, garlic, tomatoes, and peppers cooked in a bright and herby tomato sauce.

Serving: 4
Preparation time: 20 minutes
Ready time: 40 minutes

Ingredients:
- 1-2 tablespoons extra-virgin olive oil
- 1 onion, diced
- 2 cloves garlic, minced
- 1 eggplant, diced into small cubes
- 2 zucchini, diced into small cubes
- 2 bell peppers (any color), diced
- 2 tablespoons fresh basil, chopped
- 2 tablespoons fresh thyme leaves, chopped
- 1/2 teaspoon of ground cumin
- 2 cups diced & peeled tomatoes
- 1/2 teaspoon sea salt
- 1/2 teaspoon freshly ground black pepper

Instructions:

1. In a large skillet heat the oil over medium-high heat. Add the onion and garlic and cook for 3-4 minutes until softened.
2. Add the diced eggplant, zucchini, and bell peppers to the skillet. Cook for an additional 5-7 minutes until all the vegetables have softened and are lightly browned.
3. Stir in the chopped fresh basil and thyme, cumin, diced tomatoes, salt, and pepper. Bring to a simmer over medium-low heat and cook for an additional 10-15 minutes.
4. Taste and adjust seasonings if needed. Serve warm.

Nutrition information:
Calories: 229 kcal, Carbohydrates: 38 g, Protein: 7 g, Fat: 6 g, Saturated Fat: 1 g, Sodium: 412 mg, Potassium: 1438 mg, Fiber: 13 g, Sugar: 11 g, Vitamin A: 5565 IU, Vitamin C: 195 mg, Calcium: 87 mg, Iron: 4 mg

6. Beef Wellington

Beef Wellington is a British classic, made of beef steak, mushrooms, and red wine, encased in puff pastry. This is a delicious dish that is perfect to serve at special occasions or dinner parties.
Serving: 6
Preparation Time: 40 minutes
Ready Time: 1 hour 40 minutes

Ingredients:
- 600g-700g puff pastry
- 4 thyme sprigs
- 2 tablespoons olive oil
- 2 shallots
- 1 clove garlic
- 800g lean beef steak
- 300g chestnut mushrooms
- 150ml dry red wine
- 3 tablespoons grainy mustard
- 1 egg, beaten

Instructions:
1. Preheat the oven to 220°C/200°C fan/gas mark 7.

2. Cut a 30x40cm rectangle from the pastry and brush with a little of the beaten egg. Place the thyme in rows along the middle of the pastry and cut two vertical slices in the pastry so it can fold over the thyme. Cook in the oven for 12 minutes until golden.

3. Heat the oil in a large saucepan and cook the shallots and garlic until soft.

4. Add the steak and mushrooms and cook until the steak is browned.

5. Pour the wine into the pan, stir in the mustard and cook for 2 minutes.

6. Remove the steak and mushrooms and allow to cool slightly before placing on the pastry.

7. Cut another piece of pastry in the same size as the first one and place on top. Crimp the edges together with a fork.

8. Glaze the top with the remaining beaten egg and cook for 30 minutes until golden.

Nutrition information: (Per Serving)
- 286 Calories
- 13.3g Fat
- 2.9g Sat Fat
- 18.1g Protein
- 8.2g Carbs
- 1.3g Fiber

7. Chicken Cordon Bleu

Chicken Cordon Bleu is an easy recipe that makes a simple and delicious dish by stuffing a chicken breast with ham and cheese.
Serving: Serves 4
Preparation Time: 10 minutes
Ready Time: 45 minutes

Ingredients:
- 4 boneless, skinless chicken breasts
- 8 thin slices cooked ham
- 4 slices Swiss or provolone cheese
- ¼ cup all-purpose flour
- 2 eggs, beaten
- 2 tablespoons water

- 2/3 cup bread crumbs
- 3 tablespoons butter

Instructions:
1. Preheat the oven to 375 degrees Fahrenheit
2. Use a mallet to flatten the chicken breasts. Place a slice of ham and a slice of cheese on each chicken breast, and roll the breast up and secure it with toothpicks.
3. Place the flour in a shallow dish. In another shallow dish, mix together the eggs and water. In a third shallow dish, add the bread crumbs and mix together.
4. Dip each chicken roll in the flour, then in the egg mixture, and then in the bread crumbs, coating each roll completely.
5. Place the chicken rolls in a greased baking dish, and top with butter.
6. Bake in the oven at 375 degrees Fahrenheit for 40-45 minutes, until chicken is cooked and juices run clear.

Nutrition information: Calories 441; Protein 41g; Total fat 18g; Cholesterol 140mg; Sodium 867mg; Total carbohydrates 28g; Fiber 1g; Sugar 3g.

8. Eggs Benedict

Eggs Benedict is a popular breakfast dish of poached eggs and Canadian bacon or ham on English muffins, topped with hollandaise sauce.
Serving: 2
Preparation time: 10 mins
Ready time: 10 mins

Ingredients:
- 2 English muffins, split
- 2 eggs
- 2 slices of Canadian bacon or ham
- 2 tablespoons of butter
- 2 tablespoons of white vinegar
- 2 tablespoons of hollandaise sauce

Instructions:

15

:
1. Preheat oven to 375°F (190°C).
2. Place the English muffins in the oven to toast for 5 minutes or until lightly browned.
3. Heat the butter in a small saucepan over medium heat until melted.
4. Add the eggs to the butter and cook over medium-low heat for 2 minutes.
5. Add the bacon or ham to the pan and cook for an additional 2 minutes, flipping the eggs occasionally.
6. Assemble the Benedict: Place the muffins on a plate and top with a cooked egg, bacon or ham, and hollandaise sauce.

Nutrition information:
Calories: 385 | Carbohydrates: 30g | Protein: 19g | Fat: 20g | Saturated Fat: 7g | Cholesterol: 305mg | Sodium: 930mg | Potassium: 253mg | Fiber: 2g | Sugar: 1g | Vitamin A: 295IU | Calcium: 148mg | Iron: 2mg

9. Paella

Paella is a traditional Spanish dish that is prepared with rice, vegetables, meat, seafood, and spices. It is known for its savory flavor and colorful presentation. It is typically served as the main course of a meal.
Serving: Serves 4
Preparation Time: 10 minutes
Ready Time: 45 minutes

Ingredients:
- 2 tablespoons olive oil
- 1 onion, diced
- 2 cloves garlic, minced
- 1 cup long-grain white rice
- 2 cups chicken stock
- 1 teaspoon smoked paprika
- 1 teaspoon turmeric
- 1 red bell pepper, diced
- 1 cup frozen peas
- 1/4 cup chopped parsley
- 2 tablespoons chopped chorizo

- 1/2 teaspoon saffron threads
- 8 ounces shrimp, peeled and deveined
- 8 ounces mussels, scrubbed and debearded
- Juice of 1 lemon

Instructions:
1. Heat the olive oil in a large saucepan over medium heat. Add the onion and garlic and cook until softened, about 5 minutes.
2. Add the rice, chicken stock, paprika, and turmeric. Bring to a simmer and cook for 15 minutes.
3. Add the bell pepper, peas, parsley, chorizo, and saffron. Simmer for another 10 minutes.
4. Add the shrimp and mussels. Cover the pan and simmer for 5 minutes, or until the shrimp and mussels are cooked through.
5. Squeeze the lemon juice into the paella and serve.

Nutrition information: (per serving): 477 calories; 17.3g fat; 30.3g carbohydrate; 3.8g fiber; 53.8g protein

10. Baked Alaska

Baked Alaska, also known as an omelet norvegienne or omelette norvegienne, is an iconic dessert comprised of ice cream and meringue, baked until the meringue is golden-brown.
Serving: 8-10 servings.
Preparation Time: 20 minutes
Ready Time: 1 hour

Ingredients:
- 2 ½ cups heavy cream
- ½ cup light corn syrup
- 6 egg yolks
- 1 teaspoon vanilla
- 2 cups they ice cream, softened
- 6 egg whites
- ¼ teaspoon cream of tartar
- ½ cup granulated sugar

Instructions:

1. Preheat oven to 475°F.

2. In a medium saucepan, whisk together the heavy cream, corn syrup, egg yolks, and vanilla. Heat over medium heat until the mixture begins to thicken and coat the back of a spoon. Remove from heat and set aside.

3. In a large bowl, beat the softened ice cream until smooth. Pour the cooled cream mixture into the ice cream and stir until well-combined.

4. In a medium bowl, beat the egg whites and cream of tartar until frothy. Gradually add the sugar while continuing to beat until stiff peaks form.

5. Gently fold the egg whites into the ice cream mixture until evenly distributed.

6. Place the mixture into an ungreased 9-inch round cake pan. Bake for 15 minutes, or until the meringue is lightly browned.

7. Allow the baked Alaska to cool slightly before serving.

Nutrition information: 90 calories, 9g fat, 5g carbohydrates, 2g protein, 0g dietary fiber, 30mg cholesterol, 37mg sodium.

11. Beef Stroganoff

Beef Stroganoff is a classic, comforting dish made with tender pieces of beef and mushrooms cooked in a creamy, tangy sauce.

Serving: 4
Preparation Time: 10 minutes
Ready Time: 40 minutes

Ingredients:
- 2 tablespoons vegetable oil
- 1 pound steak tenderloin or sirloin, cut into thin strips
- 8 ounces cremini mushrooms, sliced
- 2 cloves garlic, minced
- 1 tablespoon tomato paste
- ½ teaspoon dried thyme
- 2 tablespoons all-purpose flour
- 1 cup beef stock
- ¾ cup sour cream
- 2 tablespoons finely chopped fresh parsley

• Salt and pepper to taste

Instructions:
1. Heat the oil in a large skillet over medium-high heat.
2. Once hot, add the steak and cook until lightly browned, about 3 minutes.
3. Add the mushrooms, garlic, tomato paste, and thyme to the skillet and cook until the mushrooms are just starting to soften, about 4 minutes.
4. Sprinkle the flour over the mixture and cook for about 1 minute.
5. Add the beef stock and stir to combine. Bring the mixture to a simmer and cook for about 5 minutes, stirring occasionally.
6. Stir in the sour cream and let the mixture simmer for a few minutes, until thickened.
7. Remove the skillet from the heat and stir in the parsley. Season with salt and pepper to taste.

Nutrition information:
Calories: 250,Fat: 16 g,Carbohydrates: 8 g,Protein: 21 g,Sodium: 390 mg

12. Chicken Parmesan

Chicken Parmesan is a classic Italian-American dish loved by all. The combination of fried chicken topped with cheese and a savory tomato sauce makes for an irresistible entree. Serve inspired Italian flavors with this easy 10-step recipe.
Serving: 4
Preparation Time: 20 minutes
Ready Time: 30 minutes

Ingredients:
- 4 skinless, boneless chicken breasts
- 2 eggs, beaten
- 1 cup all-purpose flour
- 2 cups breadcrumbs
- 1 teaspoon garlic powder
- 2 teaspoons Italian seasoning
- 1 teaspoon paprika
- Salt and pepper (to taste)

- 2 cups Italian blend cheese
- 2 tablespoons olive oil
- 2 cups tomato sauce

Instructions:
1. Preheat oven to 375° F.
2. To make the breadcrumb mixture, mix the breadcrumbs, garlic powder, Italian seasoning, paprika, and salt & pepper to taste in a shallow dish.
3. In another shallow dish, add the flour. Then, add the beaten eggs in a separate dish.
4. Dip the chicken breasts in the flour, then egg, and then the breadcrumb mixture, making sure each side is evenly coated.
5. Place the chicken breasts on a greased baking tray and bake for 20 minutes.
6. Heat the olive oil in a skillet over medium heat. Place the chicken breasts in the skillet and cook for 3 minutes on each side.
7. Remove the chicken from the skillet and place onto a serving platter.
8. Top with the tomato sauce and Italian blend cheese.
9. Bake in preheated oven for 10 minutes.
10. Enjoy!

Nutrition information:
Calories: 400, Total Fat: 18g, Saturated Fat: 7g, Trans Fat: 0g, Cholesterol: 145mg, Sodium: 1170mg, Total Carbohydrate: 23g, Dietary Fiber: 2g, Sugars: 5g, Protein: 33g

13. Lobster Bisque

Lobster Bisque is a creamy, smooth and rich soup with loads of nutritious lobster meat. This popular French-style seafood dish is sure to delight any seafood lover.
Serving: 4
Preparation Time: 10 minutes
Ready Time: 55 minutes

Ingredients:
• 2 tbsp butter

- 1 onion, diced
- 2 celery stalks, chopped
- 1 carrot, peeled and chopped
- 2 cloves garlic, chopped
- 2 cups seafood or fish stock
- 1 cup dry white wine
- 1/2 cup heavy cream
- 2 (1/2 lb) cooked lobster tails, cut into chunks
- 2 tbsp tomato paste
- Salt and pepper, to taste

Instructions:
1. In a large pot over medium heat, melt the butter and sauté the onion, celery, carrot and garlic for 5 minutes.
2. Add the seafood or fish stock and white wine and bring to a boil. Reduce heat to low and simmer for 30 minutes.
3. Add the cream, cooked lobster tails and tomato paste and simmer for another 10 minutes.
4. Season with salt and pepper to taste.
5. Serve the Lobster Bisque hot with garlic bread on the side.

Nutrition information: Per serving: 211 kcals, 12g fat, 4g carbohydrates, 21g protein

14. Tarte Tatin

Tarte Tatin is a French apple tart made with a flakey pastry base and a delicious caramelized apples topping.
Serving: 8
Preparation time: 30 minutes
Ready time: 45 minutes

Ingredients:
- 8-10 Braeburn apples
- 125g unsalted butter, cubed
- 125g caster sugar
- 1 x 25cm ready-made shortcrust pastry

Instructions:

1. Preheat oven to 220°C. Heat a 20cm non-stick frying pan over a medium heat. Add cubed butter and sugar and stir until melted and combined, allowing it to turn a golden caramel color.

2. Peel, core and quarter the apples and arrange them in the caramel in the frying pan. Cook for a further 10 minutes over a medium heat.

3. Roll out the pastry and place over the caramelized apples, tucking in the edges of the pastry. Place the frying pan in the hot oven for 25-30 minutes until the pastry is golden and crisp.

4. Remove from the oven, run around the inside of the frying pan with a small knife and flip onto a plate or tray. Serve warm or cool.

Nutrition information: Per serving: 226 kcal, 9.6g fat, 12.2g sugar

15. Escargots de Bourgogne

Escargots de Bourgogne is a classic French dish, traditionally made with snails cooked in garlic and parsley butter. This rich recipe is sure to impress.

Serving: 8
Preparation Time: 10 minutes
Ready Time: 45 minutes

Ingredients:
– 1/2 cup butter
– 1/2 cup minced parsley
– 3 cloves minced garlic
– 2 tablespoons white wine
– 3 dozen escargots, cooked

Instructions:
1. Preheat oven to 350 degrees F (175 degrees C).
2. In a small bowl, mix together butter, parsley, garlic, and white wine.
3. Place escargots into an oven-safe dish.
4. Cover escargots with the butter mixture.
5. Bake in preheated oven for 30 minutes, or until fully heated through.

Nutrition information:

Calories: 376 calories; Protein: 12.5g; Carbohydrates: 1.4g; Fat: 35.9g; Cholesterol: 55mg; Sodium: 188mg; Fiber: 0.1g.

16. Croque Monsieur

Croque Monsieur is a classic French sandwich made with creamy cheese, ham, and bread. It is simple and easy to make yet incredibly delicious.
Serving: Makes 2 sandwiches
Preparation time: 15 minutes
Ready Time: 15 minutes

Ingredients:
- 3 tablespoons butter, divided
- 2 slices of white sandwich bread
- 2 slices of cooked ham
- 2 slices of cheese (Edam or Gruyere cheese)
- 2 tablespoons grated Parmesan cheese
- 2 tablespoons of Dijon mustard

Instructions:
1. Preheat oven to 375°F (190°C).
2. Spread 1 tablespoon of butter on one side of each bread slice.
3. Place the 2 bread slices, butter-side-down, onto a baking sheet.
4. Put the cooked ham slices on top of the bread, followed by the cheese slices.
5. Spread the remaining butter on top of the cheese and sprinkle with Parmesan cheese.
6. Bake in the preheated oven for 10 minutes, until the cheese has melted and the bread is golden brown.
7. Take out of the oven and spread mustard over the top of each sandwich.
8. Cut the sandwiches in half and serve warm.

Nutrition information
Per serving (1 sandwich): 420 kcal, 25 g fat, 32 g carbohydrates, 4 g sugar, 21 g protein.

17. Shrimp Scampi

Shrimp Scampi is a classic Italian-American dish made with sautéed shrimp tossed in white wine, butter, garlic, lemon, and parsley.
Serving: 4
Preparation time: 15 minutes
Ready time: 20 minutes

Ingredients:
1 pound jumbo shrimp, peeled and deveined
4 tablespoons butter
2 cloves garlic, minced
1/4 cup dry white wine
1/4 teaspoon crushed red pepper flakes
Juice of 1 lemon
2 tablespoons chopped fresh parsley
Salt and pepper to taste

Instructions:
1. Heat the butter in a large skillet over medium high heat.
2. Add the garlic and sauté for about 1 minute.
3. Add the shrimp and cook until pink and opaque, about 4-5 minutes.
4. Add the wine, red pepper flakes, lemon juice, and parsley and bring to a simmer.
5. Simmer for another 4-5 minutes, stirring often.
6. Season with salt and pepper to taste.

Nutrition information:
Amount per Serving: Calories:213, Fat: 11.2g, Carbohydrates: 2g, Protein: 24.7g, Sodium: 402mg, Cholesterol: 213mg

18. Quiche Lorraine

Quiche Lorraine is a traditional French savory tarts, it is made with eggs, milk, cream, savory bacon and cheese.
Serving: 6
Preparation Time: 15 mins
Ready Time: 45 mins

Ingredients:
- 4 slices of bacon, chopped
- 1 onion, chopped
- 2 ounces of shredded gruyere or Swiss cheese
- 2 tablespoons of butter
- 1 unbaked 9-inch pie crust
- 2 eggs
- 1 cup of milk
- 1 cup of heavy cream
- Salt and pepper to taste

Instructions:
1. Preheat oven to 375 degrees F (190 degrees C).
2. Cook bacon, onion and butter in a medium skillet over medium heat until onion is tender and bacon is cooked, about 10 minutes.
3. Layer bacon and cooked onion in the bottom of the unbaked pie crust.
4. Sprinkle shredded cheese over bacon and onion.
5. Beat together eggs, milk and cream. Pour egg mixture over cheese and bacon.
6. Bake for 35 to 40 minutes, until center is firm and the quiche is golden brown.
7. Let stand for 10 minutes before serving.

Nutrition information: (per serving) 570 calories, 38g fat, 34g carbohydrates, 22g protein.

19. Beef Carpaccio

Beef Carpaccio is a delicious, thinly sliced raw beef dish topped with a drizzle of olive oil, flakes of parmesan cheese, and a pinch of salty capers.
Serving: 4
Preparation Time: 15 minutes
Ready Time: 10 minutes

Ingredients:

- 225g very thinly sliced beef fillet
- 2 tablespoons of extra-virgin olive oil
- 2 tablespoons freshly-squeezed lemon juice
- 1 tablespoon freshly-grated parmesan cheese
- Salt and freshly-ground black pepper, to taste
- 1 tablespoon capers

Instructions:
1. Slice the beef fillet as thinly as possible.
2. Arrange the beef slices over a large plate.
3. Drizzle with olive oil and lemon juice.
4. Dot the beef with parmesan cheese.
5. Season with salt and pepper, to taste.
6. Sprinkle with capers.
7. Serve with toasted ciabatta or crunchy crostini.

Nutrition information: Per serving: Calories 193, Total Fat 12g, Cholesterol 40mg, Sodium 294mg, Total Carbohydrate 3g, Protein 16g.

20. Chicken Marsala

Chicken Marsala is a delicious Italian-American dish made of chicken and mushrooms cooked in a Marsala wine sauce. This classic dish is easy to make and great for any special occasion.
Serving: 4
Preparation Time: 10 minutes
Ready Time: 25 minutes

Ingredients:
- 4 boneless, skinless chicken breasts
- 2 tablespoons vegetable oil
- 8 ounces crimini mushrooms, sliced
- 1/4 cup shallot, minced
- 2 cloves garlic, minced
- 2 cups Marsala wine
- 1/2 cup chicken broth
- 1 tablespoon fresh thyme, chopped

- 2 tablespoons butter
- 1/2 cup parsley, chopped

Instructions:
1. In a large skillet, heat the oil over medium heat. Season the chicken breasts with salt and pepper.
2. Place the chicken breasts in the skillet and cook for 8-10 minutes until it's cooked through and golden brown.
3. Move the chicken to a plate and cover with foil to keep warm.
4. Add the mushrooms to the same skillet and cook until softened, about 5 minutes.
5. Add the shallot and garlic and cook for 2 minutes more.
6. Pour in the Marsala wine and chicken broth. Stir in the thyme and bring to a boil.
7. Return the chicken to the skillet and simmer for 10 minutes until the sauce is reduced.
8. Remove the skillet from the heat and stir in the butter and parsley.

Nutrition information: Per Serving - Calories: 254, Fat: 7.9g, Carbohydrates: 9.3g, Protein: 26.8g, Sodium: 835.6mg, Fiber: 0.5g

21. Coquilles Saint-Jacques

Coquilles Saint-Jacques is a classic French dish of sea scallops poached in a delicious white wine sauce. This delightful dish is an impressive main course for a special occasion.
Serving: 4
Preparation time: 10 minutes
Ready time: 25 minutes

Ingredients:
- 2 pounds sea scallops
- 2 tablespoons unsalted butter
- 2 tablespoons white wine
- 2 tablespoons vegetable oil
- 2 tablespoons minced shallots
- 1/2 cup dry white wine
- 2 tablespoons chopped parsley

- Salt and pepper to taste

Instructions:
1. Pat the scallops dry with a paper towel and season lightly with salt and pepper.
2. Heat the oil and butter in a large skillet over medium-high heat until hot.
3. Add the scallops and sear on each side for about 2 minutes.
4. Add the shallots and cook for 1 minute, stirring frequently.
5. Pour in the white wine, stirring to scrape up any browned bits from the bottom of the pan.
6. Bring the mixture to a boil and cook for 2 minutes.
7. Reduce the heat to low and simmer for 3 minutes.
8. Stir in the parsley and season to taste with salt and pepper.
9. Serve the scallops with the sauce on the side.

Nutrition information:
-Calories - 230
-Total fats - 8.3 g
-Cholesterol – 68 mg
-Sodium – 500 mg
-Total carbs – 5.4 g
-Protein – 31.7 g

22. Eggs Florentine

Eggs Florentine is a classic brunch dish that pairs poached eggs with a creamy Mornay sauce, wilted spinach, and toasted English muffins. This dish can be served for breakfast, lunch, or dinner, and can be quickly and easily prepared.
Serving: 4
Preparation Time: 10 minutes
Ready Time: 25 minutes

Ingredients:
• 4 English muffins
• 2 tablespoons butter, melted
• 2 cups baby spinach

- 4 large eggs
- 1 ¼ cup white sauce
- ¼ cup grated Parmesan
- Salt and pepper

Instructions:
1. Preheat the oven to 350°F.
2. Toast the English muffins in the oven for 10 minutes, or until lightly browned.
3. In a medium skillet, melt the butter over medium heat and add the spinach. Cook for 3-4 minutes until wilted.
4. In a medium saucepan, prepare white sauce according to instructions.
5. Once the sauce is ready, add the Parmesan cheese and season with salt and pepper.
6. Bring a medium pot of water to a boil and add a pinch of salt. Gently crack the eggs one at a time and poach for 2-3 minutes.
7. To assemble the eggs Florentine, place two halves of an English muffin on each plate. Top with spinach, and then a poached egg. Spoon the sauce over the eggs and sprinkle with Parmesan cheese.

Nutrition information: Calories: 253, Protein: 11.5g, Fat: 14.4g, Carbohydrates: 18.4g

23. Duck à l'Orange

Duck à l'Orange is a classic French classic that adds a touch of luxury to any meal. Paired with a creamy orange sauce, its rich, succulent flavor is sure to bring out the gastronome in anyone.
Serving: 4
Preparation Time: 15 minutes
Ready Time: 50 minutes

Ingredients:
- 4 duck breasts
- 6 tablespoons butter
- 2 cloves garlic, minced
- 2 oranges, zested and juiced
- 2 tablespoons brandy
- 1 cup chicken broth

- 1 teaspoon fresh thyme leaves
- Salt and black pepper, to taste

Instructions:
1. Preheat the oven to 350 degrees F (175 degrees C).
2. Place the duck breasts on a cutting board and season with salt and pepper.
3. Heat the butter in a large skillet over medium-high heat. When the butter has melted, add the garlic and cook until fragrant, about 1 minute.
4. Add the duck breasts and cook until golden brown, 4 to 5 minutes per side. Remove the duck from the skillet and transfer to a baking dish.
5. In the remaining butter in the skillet, add the orange zest and juice, brandy, chicken broth, and thyme. Bring to a simmer and cook until the sauce has reduced by half.
6. Pour the sauce over the duck and place in the preheated oven. Bake until cooked through, about 25 minutes.
7. Remove from the oven and let rest for 5 minutes before serving.

Nutrition information: Per serving - Calories: 421, Total Fat: 27 g, Saturated Fat: 14 g, Cholesterol: 111 mg, Sodium: 241 mg, Total Carbohydrates: 5 g, Dietary Fiber: 1 g, Protein: 33 g.

24. Oysters Rockefeller

Oysters Rockefeller is a classic seafood dish that dates back to 1899. It is an impressive and elegant dish made with a delicious combination of oysters, herbs, and béchamel sauce.
Serving: 4
Preparation Time: 30 mins
Ready Time: 1 hour

Ingredients:
- 12 oysters on the half shell
- 2 tablespoons butter
- 2 cloves garlic, minced
- 1 cup spinach, finely chopped
- 1 green onion, sliced
- 3 tablespoons fresh parsley, chopped

- 1/2 teaspoon sea salt
- 1/4 teaspoon black pepper
- 1 teaspoon Worcestershire sauce
- 2 tablespoons Pernod or absinthe
- 2 tablespoons all-purpose flour
- 1 cup half-and-half cream
- 2 tablespoons Parmesan cheese, grated

Instructions:
1. Preheat the oven to 400 F.
2. In a large skillet, melt the butter over medium heat.
3. Add the garlic, spinach, green onion, parsley, salt and pepper. Sauté for 5 minutes, stirring often until the vegetables are softened.
4. Remove the skillet from the heat and stir in the Worcestershire sauce and Pernod.
5. Spoon the mixture evenly onto the oysters.
6. Place the oysters in a greased baking dish.
7. In a separate bowl, whisk together the flour and half-and-half cream until smooth. Pour the mixture over the oysters.
8. Sprinkle the Parmesan cheese on top.
9. Bake for 20 minutes, or until the sauce is bubbling and the oysters are cooked.

Nutrition information: 380 calories; 18 g fat (8 g saturated fat); 32 mg cholesterol; 706 mg sodium; 23 g carbohydrate; 3 g fiber; 8 g protein.

25. Escargot à la Bourguignonne

Escargot à la Bourguignonne is a classic French dish made with snails cooked in a wine, garlic, and parsley sauce. It is a traditional dish of Burgundy.
Serving: 4
Preparation Time: 15 minutes
Ready Time: 45-50 minutes

Ingredients:
-24-30 snails (cleaned)
-5 cloves of garlic (minced)

-2 tbsp. of parsley (chopped)
-2 tbsp. of butter
-1/2 glass dry white wine
-Salt
-Pepper

Instructions:
1. Start by cleaning the snails with water and a small brush.
2. In a large frying pan, melt the butter over medium-high heat.
3. Add the minced garlic and chopped parsley and cook until fragrant, about 1-2 minutes.
4. Pour the half glass of white wine, and let it simmer until it reduces by half.
5. Add the snails to the pan and season with salt and pepper.
6. Cook for about 10 minutes until the snails are cooked through.
7. Serve hot and enjoy!

Nutrition information: per serving, approximate:
Calories: 127; Protein: 2.7g; Fat: 10.7g; Saturated Fat: 5.7g; Carbohydrate: 2.6g; Sugar: 0.2g; Fiber: 0.2g; Cholesterol: 21mg; Sodium: 776mg.

26. Chicken Piccata

Chicken Piccata is an Italian recipe that is composed of delicate slices of chicken, covered in a light lemon-butter sauce. This delicious main course dish is perfect when served with sides such as steamed vegetables, potatoes, and boiled pasta.
Serving: Serves 4
Preparation time: 15 minutes
Ready Time
30 minutes

Ingredients:
• 2 chicken breasts, cut into thin slices
• 1/2 cup all-purpose flour
• 3 tablespoons olive oil
• Salt and black pepper to taste
• 1 tablespoon butter

- 2 cloves garlic, minced
- 1/2 cup chicken broth
- 2 tablespoons lemon juice
- 2 tablespoons capers
- 2 tablespoons chopped parsley

Instructions:
1. In a shallow bowl, combine the flour, salt, and pepper.
2. Heat the oil in a large skillet over medium heat.
3. Working in batches, coat the chicken with the flour mixture, shaking off any excess.
4. Place the chicken in the skillet and cook until it is lightly browned and cooked through, 3-4 minutes per side.
5. Remove the chicken from the skillet and set aside.
6. Add the butter to the skillet, followed by the garlic.
7. Cook for 1 minute, stirring constantly.
8. Stir in the chicken broth, lemon juice, and capers.
9. Return the chicken to the skillet and simmer until the sauce has thickened, about 5 minutes.
10. Sprinkle with parsley and serve.

Nutrition information
Calories: 283
Fat: 13g
Carbohydrates: 16g
Protein: 22g
Sugar: 2g
Fiber: 2g
Cholesterol: 70mg
Sodium: 554mg

27. Chateaubriand

Chateaubriand is a tenderloin steak that is named after the French diplomat. The steak is cut from the center of the beef tenderloin. When prepared correctly, Chateaubriand is a juicy and tender dish.
Serving: 4
Preparation time: 10 minutes

Ready time: 40 minutes

Ingredients:
- 1 beef tenderloin roast (2 to 3 lbs)
- 2 tablespoons olive oil
- 2 garlic cloves, minced
- 1 teaspoon fresh rosemary, finely chopped
- 1 teaspoon fresh thyme, finely chopped
- 1 teaspoon sea salt
- 1 teaspoon black pepper
- 2 tablespoons butter
- 2 tablespoons Worcestershire sauce

Instructions:
1. Preheat the oven to 400 degrees F.
2. In a small bowl, stir together olive oil, garlic, rosemary, thyme, sea salt, and pepper.
3. Rub the mixture all over the roast.
4. Heat a large skillet over medium-high heat. Add the butter and let it melt.
5. Once the butter starts to sizzle, place the roast in the pan. Sear it on all sides, about 2 minutes per side.
6. Pour the Worcestershire sauce over the roast and transfer the skillet to the oven.
7. Bake the roast for 25 to 30 minutes, or until it reaches an internal temperature of 145 degrees F.
8. Remove the roast from the oven and let it rest for 10 minutes.
9. Slice the Chateaubriand into 1-inch thick slices and serve.

Nutrition information: Per Serving, Calories 537 Fat 34.2g, Cholesterol 156g, Sodium 471mg, Potassium 823g, Protein 51g, Carbohydrates 3.4g, Fiber .5g, Sugar 0g.

28. Lobster Thermidor

This classic French dish features succulent lobster in a creamy white wine sauce. The dish is typically served in the lobster's shell, topped with a light sprinkle of cheese. Serves: 4 Preparation time: 30 minutes Ready in: 40 minutes

Ingredients:
2 cooked lobsters, 1.5 tablespoons of butter, 2 tablespoons of flour, 1 cup of white wine, 1/2 cup of half and half, 2 tablespoons of Dijon mustard, 1/4 teaspoon of cayenne pepper, 1/2 cup of grated Parmesan cheese

Instructions:
1. In a medium saucepan, melt the butter over low heat.
2. Add the flour and stir until it forms a paste.
3. Gradually whisk in the white wine, stirring continuously until the sauce thickens.
4. Add the half and half, Dijon mustard, and cayenne pepper and continue to stir until the sauce is smooth.
5. Transfer the sauce to a separate dish and set aside.
6. Carefully remove the meat from the lobster shells and cut into bite-size pieces.
7. Preheat the oven to 375 degrees F.
8. Place the lobster pieces in an oven-safe dish and pour the sauce over the top.
9. Sprinkle with the Parmesan cheese and bake for 15 minutes.
10. Serve immediately.

Nutrition information: Calories: 435, Total Fat: 28g, Saturated Fat: 15.2g, Cholesterol: 136mg, Sodium: 566mg, Total Carbohydrates: 17.4g, Dietary Fiber: 1.7g, Sugars: 0.4g, Protein: 24.8g

29. Bœuf à la Mode

Bœuf à la mode is a classic French stew made with beef, lardons (small cubes of bacon), button mushrooms, pearl onions, white wine, and herbs. Rich and comforting, this hearty dish is sure to be a hit with family and friends.
Serving: 6
Preparation Time: 15 minutes
Ready Time: 3 hours

Ingredients:
- 2 pounds of beef chuck, cubed
- 2 teaspoons of sea salt
- 1 teaspoon of freshly ground black pepper
- 2 tablespoons of lard or vegetable oil
- 4 ounces of lardons (small cubes of bacon)
- 1/2 pound of button mushrooms
- 1/2 pound of pearl onions
- 1 cup of white wine
- 2 cloves of garlic, minced
- 2 sprigs of fresh thyme
- 1 bay leaf

Instructions:
1. Preheat the oven to 300°F.
2. Place the cubed beef in a large bowl and season with the sea salt and freshly ground black pepper.
3. Heat the lard or vegetable oil in a large, oven-safe pot over medium-high heat and then add the beef cubes. Brown the beef cubes on all sides.
4. Add the lardons, button mushrooms, pearl onions, white wine, garlic, thyme, and bay leaf. Bring the mixture to a low simmer and then place the pot in the oven for 2 1/2 -3 hours.
5. Serve the Bœuf à la Mode over a bed of mashed potatoes or egg noodles.

Nutrition information:
Calories: 367, Fat: 17g, Saturated Fat: 6g, Carbs: 9g, Fiber: 2g, Protein: 40g, Cholesterol: 113mg, Sodium: 876mg

30. Sole Meunière

Sole Meunière is a classic French dish made with sole fillets that have been lightly coated in flour and pan-fried in butter. It is traditionally served with a lemon and caper sauce.
Serving: 4
Preparation Time: 10 minutes
Ready Time: 15 minutes

Ingredients:

- 4 sole fillets
- ¼ cup all-purpose flour
- 1 teaspoon salt
- ¼ teaspoon ground black pepper
- 3 tablespoons butter
- 2 tablespoons olive oil
- 2 tablespoons fresh lemon juice
- 2 tablespoons capers
- 2 tablespoons fresh parsley, chopped

Instructions:
1. Place the flour, salt, and pepper in a shallow bowl and mix to combine.
2. Dredge each sole fillet in the flour mixture, shaking off any excess.
3. Heat the butter and oil in a large skillet over medium-high heat.
4. Add the sole fillets and cook for 3-4 minutes on each side, or until golden brown and cooked through.
5. Remove the sole from the skillet and keep warm.
6. In the same skillet, cook the lemon juice, capers and parsley for 1 minute.
7. Pour the sauce onto the plate and top with the sole fillets.

Nutrition information: Per Serving: Calories: 261 kCal, Protein: 23g, Total Fat: 16g, Saturated Fat: 8g, Monounsaturated Fat: 5g, Carbohydrates: 7g, Sugar: 1g, Fiber: 1g, Cholesterol: 53mg, Sodium: 456mg

31. French Onion Soup

This French Onion Soup is a delicious and savory soup, with stewed onions, garlic, and herbs simmered in a decadent base of beef stock. The overall flavor is then enhanced with a sprinkling of shredded cheese on top. Perfect for any cold evening!
Serving: Serves 4.
Preparation time: 20 minutes.
Ready time: 40 minutes.

Ingredients:
-4 large onions, sliced

-4 cloves of garlic, minced
-4 tablespoons of butter
-2 tablespoons of olive oil
-2 tablespoons of all-purpose flour
-2 tablespoons of fresh thyme leaves
-6 cups of beef stock
-Salt and freshly ground pepper, to taste
-⅓ cup of freshly grated Parmesan cheese

Instructions:
1. Heat the butter and olive oil in a large stockpot over medium-high heat.
2. Add the onions and garlic and cook, stirring frequently, until the onions are softened and lightly golden, about 15 minutes.
3. Add the flour and thyme and cook for another 2 minutes.
4. Pour the beef stock into the pot and bring to a boil.
5. Reduce the heat and simmer for 20 minutes.
6. Season with salt and pepper, to taste.
7. Ladle the soup into four bowls and top with a sprinkle of Parmesan cheese.

Nutrition information: Each bowl of French Onion Soup contains approximately 100 calories, 6 grams of fat, 8 grams of carbohydrates, and 5 grams of protein.

32. Bouillabaisse Marseillaise

Bouillabaisse Marseillaise is a hearty fish stew, originating in the Mediterranean port of Marseille. Full of flavor, it's an excellent main course for any meal.
Serving: 8
Preparation time: 20 minutes
Ready time: 2 hours

Ingredients:
- 4 tablespoons olive oil
- 1 large onion, peeled and diced
- 3 cloves garlic, peeled and minced

- 2 medium carrots, peeled and diced
- 2 stalks celery, diced
- 2 tablespoons tomato paste
- 1 (14-ounce) can diced tomatoes
- 1 teaspoon fennel seeds
- 2 teaspoons dried oregano
- 1 teaspoon dried thyme
- 1 teaspoon saffron threads
- 4 cups fish stock
- 1 (1-pound) Spanish mackerel, skinned and cut into 2-inch pieces
- 1 pound monkfish, skinned and cut into 2-inch pieces
- 1 dozen mussels, cleaned and debearded
- 1 (6-ounce) can tomato sauce
- Salt and freshly ground black pepper, to taste
- 1/2 cup chopped fresh parsley

Instructions:
1. Heat the olive oil in a large pot over medium heat. Add the onion and garlic and cook until softened, about 8 minutes.
2. Add the carrots and celery and cook for 3 minutes. Stir in the tomato paste, diced tomatoes, fennel seeds, oregano, thyme, and saffron. Cook for 2 minutes.
3. Add the fish stock and bring to a boil. Reduce the heat and simmer for 30 minutes.
4. Add the mackerel, monkfish, mussels, and tomato sauce and simmer for 20 minutes, until the fish is cooked through.
5. Season with salt and pepper, to taste. Stir in the chopped parsley and serve.

Nutrition information: Per serving (8 servings): 249 calories, 13 g fat, 5 g carbohydrates, 22 g protein

33. Tournedos Rossini

Tournedos Rossini is an Italian-style beef dish made by pan-frying beef medallions and topping them with a decadent combination of savoury foie gras and truffle sauce.

Serving: 6
Preparation time: 20 minutes
Ready time: 40 minutes

Ingredients:
- 6 tournedos medallions (beef steaks cut from the fillet)
- 12 ounces foie gras
- 3 tablespoons butter
- 1/2 cup dry white wine
- 1/4 cup cream
- 1/2 cup truffle sauce
- Salt and pepper, to taste

Instructions:
1. Preheat the oven to 400 degrees F.
2. Season the tournedos medallions with salt and pepper.
3. Heat the butter in a large skillet over medium-high heat.
4. Add the tournedos medallions and cook for 2 minutes per side, or until well-browned.
5. Transfer the medallions to a baking sheet and place in the preheated oven. Bake for 8 minutes, or until cooked to desired doneness.
6. Meanwhile, heat the foie gras in a separate skillet. Cook for 2 minutes per side, or until lightly browned.
7. Add the white wine to the skillet and reduce by half.
8. Stir in the cream and heat until bubbling.
9. Taste and season with salt and pepper, as desired.
10. Top each medallion with 1 tablespoon of the foie gras and 1 tablespoon of the truffle sauce.

Nutrition information:
Serving Size: 1 tournedos medallion
Calories: 446
Fat: 28 g
Carbohydrates: 2 g
Protein: 42 g
Sodium: 464 mg

34. Pot-au-Feu

Pot-au-Feu is a classic French stew made from beef and vegetables. Originating from the Latin term Platea Fossa, meaning "pit of boiling", Pot-au-Feu is a traditional peasant dish that is sure to satisfy the whole family.
Serving : 8-10 people
Preparation Time : 15 minutes
Ready Time : 3.5 hours

Ingredients:
- 2 kg piece of Boneless Beef Shank
- 8 Quarts Water
- 2 Carrots
- 2 Onions
- 2 Celery Stalks
- 4 Cloves Garlic
- 2 Bay Leaves
- 2 tsp Salt
- 2 tsp Black Pepper
- 2 Turnips
- 2 Leeks
- 4 Parsnips
- 2 Tomatoes

Instructions:
1. In a large stock pot, add the beef shank, 8 quarts of water, carrots, onions, celery stalks, garlic cloves, bay leaves, salt, and pepper.
2. Bring the pot to a boil, reduce the heat to low, and simmer for 3 hours.
3. After 3 hours, add the turnips, leeks, parsnips, and tomatoes to the pot. Simmer for an additional 30 minutes.
4. Remove the beef shank from the pot and place on a cutting board. Skim the fat off the top of the stock, season with salt and pepper to taste.
5. Cut the beef shank into 8-10 portions. Serve on a plate with vegetables and broth from the pot.

Nutrition information:

Calories: 411 kcal, Carbohydrates: 19g, Protein: 35g, Fat: 19g, Saturated Fat: 8g, Cholesterol: 105mg, Sodium: 634mg, Potassium: 1020mg, Fiber: 3g, Sugar: 6g, Vitamin A: 2888IU, Vitamin C: 12mg, Calcium: 55mg, Iron: 4mg

35. Pissaladière

Pissaladière is a traditional Provençal tart made with thin crusty pastry, onions, olives, anchovies, and sometimes other flavorful Ingredients. It's the perfect appetizer or lunch, and can be served either hot or cold.
Serving: 8
Preparation Time: 1 hour
Ready Time: 1 hour and 20 minutes

Ingredients:
- 2 tablespoons olive oil
- 2 large onions, thinly sliced
- 2 cloves garlic, minced
- 1 teaspoon dried thyme
- 2 teaspoons sea salt
- 2 tablespoons balsamic vinegar
- 12 anchovy fillets, rinsed and chopped
- 2 tablespoons sliced black olives
- 1 sheet puff pastry, thawed
- 4 ounces goat cheese, crumbled

Instructions:
1. Preheat the oven to 375F.
2. Heat the olive oil in a large skillet over medium heat. Add the onions and garlic and sauté until the onions are soft and golden, about 10 minutes.
3. Add the thyme, salt, and balsamic vinegar and cook for 5 minutes more.
4. Spread the onion mixture in the bottom of a 9-inch tart pan.
5. Top the onions with the anchovies, olives, and puff pastry. Bake for 25 minutes.
6. Remove from the oven and sprinkle the goat cheese on top. Bake for an additional 10 minutes.
7. Let the pissaladière cool for 10 minutes before serving.

Nutrition information: Per serving: 200 calories, 12g fat, 8g saturated fat, 15g carbohydrate, 2g dietary fiber, 5g protein.

36. Croque Madame

Croque Madame is a classic French grilled ham and cheese sandwich recipe with a delicious twist - a fried egg on top. It makes an easy and elegant breakfast or brunch recipe that can be enjoyed any time of the day.

Serving: 2
Preparation time: 15 minutes
Ready time: 10 minutes

Ingredients:
- 4 slices of bread
- 2 tablespoons of butter
- 2 tablespoons of all-purpose flour
- 1 cup of milk
- 2 tablespoons of Dijon mustard
- 4 slices of cooked ham
- 4 slices of Gruyère cheese
- 2 eggs

Instructions:
1. Preheat the oven to 400 degrees F (200 degrees C).
2. Spread the butter on one side of each slice of bread and place them in a baking pan, buttered side up.
3. In a saucepan, heat the flour and milk over medium-high heat, stirring constantly until the mixture thickens.
4. Spread the mustard over the slices of bread and top with the ham, then the cheese.
5. Pour the thickened milk mixture over the top of the sandwiches; this will help make them moist and flavorful.
6. Bake in the preheated oven for 10 minutes.
7. Meanwhile, heat a non-stick pan and melt a bit of butter. Carefully break two eggs into the hot pan and cook to desired doneness.
8. When the sandwiches are done baking, top them with the fried eggs.

Nutrition information:
Calories: 432 kcal; Total Fat: 24.7 g; Saturated Fat: 11.6 g; Cholesterol: 211 mg; Sodium: 922 mg; Carbohydrates: 25.6 g; Fiber: 1.8 g; Sugar: 5.2 g; Protein: 21.7 g.

37. Bouillabaisse à la Provençale

Bouillabaisse à la Provençale is a fish stew or soup that has its origins in Marseilles, France. It is made of several varieties of fish, vegetables, and a delicious broth that elevates it above other fish stews.
Serving: 6
Preparation Time: 25 minutes
Ready Time: 1 hour

Ingredients:
2 tablespoons olive oil, 2 cloves garlic, minced, 1 onion, diced, 2 carrots, diced, 2 celery stalks, diced, 1 cup dry white wine, 2 pounds mixed fish, including monkfish, cod, red snapper, mussels, scallops, 1 can (28 ounces) diced tomatoes, 4 cups clam juice or fish stock, 2 teaspoons dried thyme, 2 teaspoons dried oregano, 2 teaspoons paprika, 3 tablespoons chopped fresh parsley, 1 lemon, juiced, Salt and freshly ground black pepper

Instructions:
1. Heat the oil in a large pot over medium heat. Add the garlic, onion, carrots, and celery and cook until softened, about 5 minutes.
2. Add the wine, fish, tomatoes, clam juice, thyme, oregano, and paprika and bring to a boil. Lower the heat and simmer for 20 minutes.
3. Stir in the parsley and lemon juice and season with salt and pepper to taste. Simmer for another 10 minutes.
4. Serve the stew in bowls with crusty bread.

Nutrition information: calories: 486, fat: 15.6 g, saturated fat: 2.6 g, cholesterol: 64 mg, sodium: 526 mg, carbohydrates: 21.9 g, fiber: 3.6 g, protein: 36.3 g, sugars: 7.5 g

38. Coq au Riesling

Coq au Riesling is an elegant and classic French dish, featuring a creamy white wine sauce made with aromatics, mushrooms, and fresh herbs over seared chicken. It is a savory, comforting, and delicious meal that can be enjoyed with a variety of sides.

Serving: 6
Preparation time: 20 minutes
Ready time: 1 hour

Ingredients:
- 6 chicken thighs and/or breasts, bone-in and skin-on
- Kosher salt and freshly ground black pepper
- 2 tablespoons olive oil
- 4 slices bacon, finely chopped
- 1 onion, finely diced
- 2 cloves garlic, minced
- 2 cups Riesling or other white wine
- 4 tablespoons unsalted butter
- 8 ounces crimini mushrooms, thinly sliced
- 2 tablespoons fresh thyme leaves
- 1/4 cup chopped fresh parsley

Instructions:
1. Heat the oven to 350 degrees F.
2. Season the chicken thighs with salt and pepper, and heat the olive oil in a large oven-safe skillet over medium-high heat.
3. Place the chicken in the skillet and cook until the skin is golden and crispy, about 7 minutes per side.
4. Remove the chicken from the skillet and set aside.
5. Add the bacon to the skillet and cook until it is crispy, about 3 minutes.
6. Add the onion and garlic and cook until the onion is softened, about 5 minutes.
7. Add the Riesling and scrape up any browned bits from the bottom of the pan.
8. Bring the mixture to a simmer and cook until it is reduced by half, about 10 minutes.
9. Add the butter, mushrooms, and thyme, and cook until the mushrooms are softened, about 5 minutes.

10. Return the chicken to the skillet and spoon the sauce over the top.
11. Place the skillet in the oven and bake for 25 minutes, or until the chicken is cooked through and the sauce is bubbling.
12. Sprinkle the parsley over top and serve.

Nutrition information: 308 calories, 19.2g fat, 9.9g carbohydrate, 18.9g protein

39. Boeuf Bourguignon

Boeuf Bourguignon is a classic French beef stew that is flavored with red Burgundy wine, bacon, and mushrooms.
Serving: Serves 8 people
Preparation time: 10 minutes
Ready time: 3 hours

Ingredients:
- 4 slices of thick cut bacon, diced
- 2 tablespoon of olive oil
- 2 - 3 lb beef top round roast, cut into 1-inch cubes
- 2 large onion, diced
- 4 cloves garlic, minced
- 2 large carrots, sliced
- 2 tablespoons of tomato paste
- 2 tablespoons of all purpose flour
- 1 bottle of dry red Burgundy wine
- 4 cups of beef broth
- 2 tablespoons of fresh thyme leaves
- 1 tablespoon of fresh rosemary leaves
- 12 ounces of button mushrooms, quartered
- 2 tablespoons of butter
- Salt and pepper to taste

Instructions:
1. Heat a large, heavy-bottomed pot over medium-high heat. Add the bacon and cook for about 5 minutes, stirring occasionally, until it is lightly browned and crisp.

2. Add the olive oil to the pot and add the beef cubes. Sear for 3 minutes each side, then remove the beef from the pot and set aside.

3. Reduce the heat to medium and add the onions, garlic, and carrots. Cook for 3 minutes, stirring occasionally, until the onions are soft.

4. Return the beef to the pot and add the tomato paste and flour. Stir to combine and cook for 2 minutes, until the flour is lightly toasted.

5. Slowly pour in the wine, stirring constantly, and bring the mixture to a boil.

6. Add the beef broth, thyme, and rosemary, and stir to combine. Reduce the heat to low, cover the pot, and simmer for 1 1/2 hours, until the beef is fork tender.

7. Add the mushrooms to the pot and stir to combine. Simmer, uncovered, for an additional 30 minutes.

8. Remove the pot from the heat and add the butter. Stir to combine and season with salt and pepper to taste.

Nutrition information: Per serving: 290 calories, 13.5g fat, 4g saturated fat, 8.5g carbohydrates, 2.1g fiber, 27.6g protein.

40. Poulet à l'Estragon

Poulet à l'Estragon is a delicious French dish made with chicken, cream, and tangy tarragon. This creamy, savory dish is sure to tantalize any palate.
Serving: Serves 4
Preparation time: 10 minutes
Ready time: 20 minutes

Ingredients:
-4 chicken breasts
-2 tablespoons butter
-2 tablespoons olive oil
-2 cloves minced garlic
-2 tablespoons chopped shallots
-1 cup dry white wine
-1 cup heavy cream
-3 tablespoons chopped fresh tarragon

Instructions:

1. In a large saucepan, melt butter with olive oil over medium heat.
2. Add the garlic and shallots and sauté until fragrant, about 2 minutes.
3. Add the chicken breasts to the pan and cook until lightly browned on each side.
4. Add the white wine and simmer for 2 minutes.
5. Add the heavy cream and tarragon and bring to a simmer.
6. Simmer for 10 minutes, until the chicken is cooked through and the sauce has thickened.
7. Serve with mashed potatoes or crusty French bread.

Nutrition information (per serving): calories: 510, fat: 25g, protein: 44g, carbohydrates: 8g, fiber: 2g, sodium: 295mg

41. Escargot à la Provençale

Escargot à la Provençale is a French appetizer or side dish made from snails cooked in a tomato butter sauce with herbs, seasonings, white wine and garlic. It is a savory dish that can be served as an appetizer with crusty French bread or as a side dish for a main course.
Serving: 4
Preparation time: 20 minutes
Ready time: 40 minutes

Ingredients:
• 12 large snails
• 2 tablespoons olive oil
• 3 cloves of garlic, chopped
• 1/2 cup white wine
• 2 tablespoons butter
• 2 tablespoons tomato paste
• 2 tablespoons freshly chopped parsley
• 2 tablespoons freshly chopped basil
• 1 teaspoon fresh thyme leaves
• 1 bay leaf
• Salt and pepper to taste

Instructions:
1. Preheat the oven to 375 degrees F.

2. Heat the oil in an ovenproof skillet over medium heat and add the snails. Cook the snails until they are lightly browned, about 10 minutes.
3. Add the garlic, white wine, butter, tomato paste, parsley, basil, thyme and bay leaf. Season to taste with salt and pepper. Cook for an additional 10 minutes.
4. Place the skillet in the preheated oven and bake for 15 minutes.
5. Serve the Escargot à la Provençale hot with fresh French bread.

Nutrition information
calories: 265
fat: 17g
saturated fat: 7g
cholesterol: 9mg
sodium: 319mg
carbohydrates: 4g
fiber: 2g
sugar: 2g
protein: 11g

42. Ratatouille Niçoise

Ratatouille Niçoise is a classic French dish that is filled with delicious flavors from eggplant, zucchini, tomatoes, garlic, and herbs. It's perfect for any summer meal and is easy to make.
Serving: 8 servings
Preparation Time: 15 minutes
Ready Time: 45 minutes

Ingredients:
- 2 tablespoons extra-virgin olive oil
- 1 medium onion, diced
- 2 cloves garlic, minced
- 2 medium eggplants, diced
- 2 zucchini, diced
- 2 bell peppers, diced
- 2 tomatoes, diced
- 1 teaspoon dried oregano
- 1 teaspoon dried thyme
- 1 teaspoon dried rosemary

- Salt and freshly ground black pepper to taste
- 2 tablespoons chopped fresh parsley

Instructions:
1. Heat the olive oil in a large skillet over medium heat.
2. Add the onion and garlic and cook until the onion is softened, about 5 minutes.
3. Add the eggplant, zucchini, bell peppers, tomato, and herbs.
4. Cook, stirring occasionally, until the vegetables are tender, about 30 minutes.
5. Season with salt and pepper to taste and stir in the parsley.
6. Serve hot.

Nutrition information: per serving: 75 calories; 4.4 g fat; 8.5 g carbohydrates; 2.5 g protein; 4 mg cholesterol; 114 mg sodium.

43. Blanquette de Veau

This classic French dish features tender veal stewed in a creamy white sauce. It is served over egg noodles or mashed potatoes.
Serving: 8
Preparation Time: 10 minutes
Ready Time: 1 hour and 10 minutes

Ingredients:
- 2 tablespoons olive oil
- 1 onion, finely chopped
- 2 pounds of veal stew meat, cubed
- Kosher salt and freshly ground pepper
- 8 ounces mushrooms, thickly sliced
- 6 tablespoons of butter
- 6 tablespoons of all-purpose flour
- 3 cups of chicken broth
- 1/2 cup heavy cream
- 1/4 cup white wine
- 2 tablespoons freshly minced parsley

Instructions:

1. Heat the oil in a large Dutch oven over medium heat. Add onions and cook until softened, about 5 minutes.

2. Add the veal cubes and season generously with salt and pepper. Cook until lightly browned, about 8 minutes.

3. Add the mushrooms and cook until softened, about 5 minutes.

4. Add the butter and melt. Stir in the flour and cook for one minute.

5. Whisk in chicken broth, then cream and white wine. Simmer the mixture for 30 minutes, stirring occasionally.

6. Add the parsley and adjust seasoning with salt and pepper.

Nutrition information: Calories: 351; Total Fat: 24.5 g; Saturated Fat: 10.7 g; Cholesterol: 106 mg; Sodium: 711 mg; Carbohydrates: 10.1 g; Dietary Fiber: 1.2 g; Protein: 23.3 g

44. Cassoulet

Cassoulet is a French peasant dish that is traditionally cooked with beans and any variety of meats like pork, beef, duck, and sausage. It is slow-cooked over a low flame making it a comforting and hearty meal.
Serving: 4 – 6
Preparation time: 15 minutes
Ready time: 2 – 3 hours

Ingredients:
2 cloves garlic, minced
1 onion, chopped
2 teaspoons olive oil
4 cups canned white beans, drained and rinsed
1 cup vegetable broth
1 teaspoon dried oregano
1 teaspoon dried thyme
1 teaspoon dried parsley
1 can (14.5 oz/ 411 g) diced tomatoes
3 cups cooked meat – diced ham, sausage, duck or pork
Salt and pepper to taste

Instructions:
1. Heat the olive oil in a large Dutch oven over medium-high heat.

51

2. Add the garlic and onion and cook until fragrant, about 2 minutes.
3. Add the beans, vegetable broth, oregano, thyme, and parsley.
4. Bring to a boil, then reduce heat to low and simmer for 1 hour.
5. Add the diced tomatoes and cooked meat and simmer for another hour or until the flavors are blended and the liquid is reduced.
6. Season with salt and pepper, to taste.

Nutrition information:
Calories: 250
Fat: 6g
Carbohydrate: 29g
Protein: 15g
Fiber: 8g

45. Confit de Canard

Confit de Canard is a French dish of duck prepared in its own fat by poaching the pieces and storing them afterwards in their own fat.
Serving: 4
Preparation time: 10 minutes
Ready time: 24 hours

Ingredients:
- 4 duck legs
- 4 duck thighs
- 2 cloves garlic, minced
- 2 sprigs fresh thyme
- 1 bay leaf
- 2 teaspoons salt
- 1 teaspoon freshly ground black pepper
- 3 cups duck fat

Instructions:
1. Preheat oven to 350°F.
2. In a bowl, combine garlic, thyme, bay leaf, salt, and pepper.
3. Place duck legs and thighs in an oven-safe pot or a Dutch oven. Sprinkle the garlic mixture over the duck pieces. Cover the pot with a lid or aluminum foil.

4. Bake in preheated oven for 1 hour and 45 minutes, or until duck is tender.
5. Remove duck from oven and let cool. After cooling, transfer duck pieces to a baking sheet lined with parchment paper.
6. Pour duck fat over the duck pieces, making sure they are completely submerged.
7. Transfer baking sheet to refrigerator and let duck pieces "confit" in the fat for 24 hours.

Nutrition information: Per Serving: 502 calories, 41g fat, 0g carbohydrates, 28g protein

46. Quiche Alsacienne

Quiche Alsacienne is a classic savory tart from the Alsace region of France. Made of a flaky pastry filled with Gruyere cheese, bacon, white sauce, and a hint of nutmeg, it's both delicious and comforting.
Serving: 8
Preparation Time: 25 minutes
Ready Time: 40 minutes

Ingredients:
- Homemade or pre-made flaky pastry
- 2 cups Gruyere, grated
- 6 slices bacon, chopped
- 2 cups white sauce (or Béchamel)
- A pinch of nutmeg

Instructions:
1. Preheat oven to 400°F.
2. Place the pastry dough into a tart pan and blind bake it for 10 minutes.
3. Sprinkle Gruyere cheese over the partially baked dough.
4. Add the chopped bacon and finish baking it for 15 minutes or until the crust is golden-brown and the cheese has melted.
5. Heat the white sauce (or Béchamel) on the stovetop until bubbling.
6. Pour the hot white sauce over the bacon and cheese.
7. Sprinkle with a pinch of nutmeg and bake for 10 minutes more.
8. Allow to cool for 5 minutes before serving.

Nutrition information: per serving (1/8 of tart): 487 calories, 27g fat, 20g protein, 34g carbohydrate, 101mg cholesterol.

47. Gougères

Gougères are light and airy French cheese puffs traditionally made from choux pastry and Gruyère cheese. They are perfect hors d'oeuvres for any event and are sure to impress guests with their delicious flavor.
Serving: Makes 12-15
Preparation time: 40 minutes
Ready time: 1 hour

Ingredients:
• 4 tablespoons (1/2 stick) butter
• Pinch of salt
• Pinch of ground white pepper
• 1 cup all-purpose flour
• 4 eggs
• 1/2 cup Gruyère cheese, grated
• 2 tablespoons Parmesan cheese, grated

Instructions:
1. Preheat the oven to 400°F. Line a baking sheet with parchment paper.
2. In a medium saucepan, heat the butter, 1/2 cup of water, salt, and white pepper over medium heat until the butter is melted. Add the flour all at once and stir vigorously until the mixture forms a ball and leaves the sides of the pan.
3. Remove the pan from the heat and let the mixture cool slightly. Add the eggs one at a time, stirring vigorously to combine. Fold in the Gruyère and Parmesan cheese.
4. Drop spoonfuls of the dough onto the prepared baking sheet. Bake for 20-25 minutes, or until golden brown. Let cool before serving.

Nutrition information: Per serving: 101 calories; 5.2g fat; 6.7g carbohydrates; 4g protein; 10mg cholesterol; 95mcg sodium.

48. Potage Parmentier

Potage Parmentier is a classic French soup dish that combines potatoes, onions, celery, and a flavorful broth to create a creamy, comforting soup.
Serving: 4
Preparation Time: 10 minutes
Ready Time: 45 minutes

Ingredients:
- 1/4 cup butter
- 1 medium yellow onion, diced
- 2 large stalks of celery, diced
- 2 cloves of garlic, minced
- 3 pounds potatoes, peeled and diced
- 4 cups vegetable or chicken stock
- 2 tablespoons fresh parsley, chopped
- Salt and ground black pepper, to taste

Instructions:
1. In a large pot, melt the butter over medium heat.
2. Add the onion, celery, and garlic to the melted butter and cook for 3-4 minutes until the onions are translucent.
3. Add the diced potatoes and stir to combine.
4. Pour in the stock and bring to a boil.
5. Reduce the heat and simmer for about 30 minutes until the potatoes are fork-tender.
6. Use an immersion blender to blend the soup until creamy and smooth.
7. Add the chopped parsley and season with salt and pepper to taste.
8. Serve hot.

Nutrition information:
Calories: 220, Total Fat: 6g, Sodium: 420mg, Total Carbohydrates: 36g, Dietary Fiber: 5g, Protein: 5g

49. Quenelles de Brochet

Quenelles de Brochet is a French dish made with pike that is blended into a paste and then shaped into oval or round shapes. It can be

poached, baked, or fried with a combination of olive oil and butter for added flavor.
Serving: Serves 4-6 people
Preparation time: 20 minutes
Ready time: 1 hour

Ingredients:
- 2lbs of Pike
- ½ cup of olive oil
- ½ cup of butter
- 2 cloves of garlic (optional)
- Salt and pepper

Instructions:
1. Preheat your oven to 375°F.
2. Fry the garlic (optional) in the olive oil until golden.
3. Put the pike in the food processor and blend until it forms a paste.
4. Scoop the paste out and shape it into oval or round shapes, then place them in the oven.
5. Bake the quenelles for 20 minutes.
6. In a separate pan, melt the butter and use it to fry the quenelles on both sides for about 3-4 minutes each.
7. Serve and enjoy!

Nutrition information:
Calories: 234
Carbs: 0g
Fat: 18g
Protein: 17g

50. Tarte Flambée

Tarte Flambée, also known as Flammekueche, is a traditional Alsatian-style pizza originating from the Alsace region of France. It's a thin-crust tart topped with crème fraîche, onions, and bacon.
Serving: 4
Preparation time: 25 minutes
Ready time: 30 minutes

Ingredients:
-1 sheet store-bought puff pastry
-1/2 cup crème fraîche
-2 large onions, thinly sliced
-100g bacon lardons
-Salt and pepper, to taste

Instructions:
1. Preheat oven to 220°C (425°F).
2. Place the puff pastry onto a baking tray and spread the crème fraîche over it.
3. Spread the bacon lardons and onions over the tart.
4. Season with salt and pepper, to taste.
5. Bake for 15-18 minutes or until the edges have risen and are golden brown.
6. Cut the tart into four pieces and serve.

Nutrition information: Per serving: calories: 603; fat: 33g; saturated fat: 16g; cholesterol: 92mg; sodium: 721mg; carbohydrate: 61g; fiber: 5g; sugar: 9g; protein: 17g.

51. Petits Pâtés à la Mode de Reims

Petits Pâtés à la Mode de Reims is a French classic made with pork, veal, truffles, brandy, and savory spices. This delicious pastry is traditionally served as an appetizer, although it can also be served as a main course.
Serving: 6
Preparation Time: 15 minutes
Ready Time: 35 minutes

Ingredients:
- 1/2 pound ground pork
- 1/2 pound ground veal
- 2 tablespoons brandy
- 1/2 teaspoon fresh thyme
- 2 cloves of minced garlic
- Salt and pepper to taste
- 1/4 cup grated Parmesan cheese
- 2 tablespoons fresh parsley, chopped

- 1/4 cup finely diced black truffle
- 2 tablespoons butter
- 1/2 cup all-purpose flour
- 1/4 cup heavy cream
- 2 sheets of puff pastry
- 1 egg yolk

Instructions:
1. Preheat the oven to 375 degrees F.
2. In a large bowl, combine the pork, veal, brandy, thyme, garlic, salt, pepper, Parmesan cheese, parsley, and truffle until well mixed.
3. In a small saucepan, melt the butter over medium heat and add the flour. Whisk until a paste forms then slowly add the cream while whisking continuously.
4. Return the mixture to the large bowl with the meat mixture and stir until all Ingredients are incorporated.
5. On a lightly floured surface, roll out the puff pastry large enough to cut out 6 circles.
6. Place about 2 tablespoons of the meat mixture on each circle and fold it in half. Press the edges together with the tines of a fork to seal.
7. Brush the tops of the pâtés with the egg yolk and place them on a greased baking sheet.
8. Bake for 20 minutes or until golden brown.

Nutrition information:
Serving Size: 1 paté
Calories: 220
Total Fat: 11 g
Saturated Fat: 4 g
Trans Fat: 0 g
Cholesterol: 44 mg
Sodium: 80 mg
Total Carbohydrate: 16 g
Dietary Fiber: 1 g
Sugars: 0 g
Protein: 11 g

52. Bœuf à la Bourguignonne

Bœuf à la Bourguignonne is the French version of beef stew, and it is incredibly savory and delicious. It is a classic French dish made up of beef, mushrooms, bacon, and red wine.

Serving: 4
Preparation time: 30 minutes
Ready time: 2 hours

Ingredients:
- 2 lbs. stewing beef, cubed
- 8 slices bacon, diced
- 2 onions, chopped
- 2 cloves garlic, minced
- 2 tablespoons all-purpose flour
- 1 bottle red wine
- 3 tablespoons olive oil
- 1 lb mushrooms, quartered
- 2 cups beef stock
- 2 bay leaves
- Salt and pepper, to taste

Instructions:
1. Heat the olive oil in a large pot over medium heat. Add the bacon and cook until it is crispy.
2. Add the onions and cook until they are softened. Add the garlic and cook until fragrant.
3. Add the beef cubes and cook until lightly browned.
4. Add the flour and stir until everything is evenly coated. Cook for 1 minute.
5. Add the red wine and beef stock and stir to combine. Add bay leaves and season with salt and pepper.
6. Increase the heat to high and bring to a boil. Reduce heat to low and let simmer, covered, for 1.5 hours.
7. Add mushrooms and continue cooking, uncovered, for 30 minutes.

Nutrition information: Calories 460, Total fat 19g, Saturated fat 7g, Sodium 460mg, Total carbohydrate 17g, Protein 27g

53. Poule au Pot

Poule au Pot is a traditional French dish consisting of a poached chicken that is cooked in a bouillon flavored with vegetables. It is a classic comfort food that is usually served with vegetables.

Serving: 4
Preparation Time: 10 minutes
Ready Time: 1 hour 30 minutes

Ingredients:
- 1 whole chicken
- 2 tablespoons of olive oil
- 1 onion, peeled and chopped
- 2 carrots, peeled and chopped
- 2 celery ribs, chopped
- 2 cloves of garlic, sliced
- 2 tablespoons of fresh thyme leaves
- 5 cups of chicken broth
- 2 bay leaves
- Salt and pepper, to taste

Instructions:
1. Preheat the oven to 350°F.
2. Rub the chicken with the olive oil and season with salt and pepper.
3. Heat a large pot or Dutch oven over medium heat and add the onion, carrots, celery, garlic, and thyme.
4. Cook until the vegetables are soft, about 5 minutes.
5. Add the chicken broth, bay leaves, and chicken.
6. Bring to a simmer, and then reduce the heat to low. Cover and cook for 1 hour and 20 minutes, until the chicken is cooked through.
7. Remove the chicken from the pot and transfer it to a serving plate. Discard the bay leaves.
8. Strain the cooking liquid and season to taste with salt and pepper.
9. Serve the chicken with the cooking liquid and vegetables.

Nutrition information: Calories: 242, Fat: 11 g, Carbs: 5 g, Protein: 28 g, Sodium: 335 mg

54. Soupe à l'Oignon Gratinée

Soupe à l'Oignon Gratinée, also known as Onion soup gratinée, is an iconic French soup made with caramelized onions, beef broth, and croutons or baguette slices topped with gooey melted cheese.

Serving: 4
Preparation Time: 15 minutes
Ready Time: 40 minutes

Ingredients:
- 3 tablespoons butter
- 2 large yellow onions, thinly sliced
- Salt, pepper, and sugar to taste
- 2 tablespoons all-purpose flour
- 4 cups beef broth
- 2 teaspoons dried thyme leaves
- 4 slices of baguette or croutons
- 1 cup shredded Gruyère or Swiss cheese

Instructions:
1. Heat butter in a large pot or Dutch oven over medium-low heat. Add the onions and season with salt, pepper, and a pinch of sugar. Cook, stirring occasionally, until the onions are very soft and lightly browned, 15 to 20 minutes.
2. Sprinkle the flour over the onions and stir to combine. Slowly add the beef broth, stirring constantly, until everything is combined and the soup is slightly thickened.
3. Add the thyme leaves and bring the soup to a simmer. Taste and adjust the seasonings if needed. Simmer for 20 minutes.
4. Arrange the bread slices on top of the soup and sprinkle the cheese evenly over them. Increase the heat to medium-high and cook until the cheese is melted and bubbling, about 8 minutes.

Nutrition information: Serving size (1 bowl): Calories: 221 kcal, Total Fat: 11 g, Saturated Fat: 6 g, Cholesterol: 30 mg, Sodium: 813 mg, Carbohydrates: 18 g, Dietary Fiber: 2 g, Sugar: 4 g, Protein: 13 g

55. Rognons de Veau à la Moutarde

Rognons de Veau à la Moutarde is a classic French dish of veal kidneys smothered in a creamy mustard sauce. It is an elegant dinner choice for any occasion.
Serving: 4
Preparation time: 10 minutes
Ready time: 25 minutes

Ingredients:
- 4 veal kidneys
- 2 tablespoons butter
- 2 tablespoons olive oil
- 1 finely chopped onion
- 400ml fresh chicken stock
- 100ml double cream
- 1 tablespoon Dijon mustard
- Fresh parsley, to garnish

Instructions:
1. Slice the veal kidneys into thin strips.
2. Heat the butter and oil in a large skillet. Add the onions and sauté until they turn golden brown.
3. Add the kidneys to the skillet and cook for 10 minutes, stirring occasionally.
4. Pour in the chicken stock and bring to a boil. Reduce the heat and simmer for 10 minutes.
5. Stir in the cream and mustard and simmer for an additional 5 minutes.
6. Garnish with parsley and serve immediately.

Nutrition information: Per Serving: 277 calories; 20 g fat; 7 g saturated fat; 7 g carbohydrates;2 g dietary fiber; 22 g protein.

56. Salade Niçoise

Salade Niçoise is a popular and flavorful French salad made with fresh Ingredients. It is often served as a starter, but is also hearty enough to stand alone as a light meal.
Serving: 4 people
Preparation time: 20 minutes
Ready time: 20 minutes

Ingredients:
- 4 eggs
- 8 ounces of green beans
- 1 head of Boston lettuce
- 2 bell peppers (1 orange, 1 yellow)
- 8 ounces of cherry tomatoes
- 2 cans of tuna in water
- 12 ounces of black olives
- 4 tablespoons of olive oil
- 4 tablespoons of white wine vinegar
- 1 teaspoon of salt
- 1 teaspoon of freshly cracked black pepper

Instructions:
1. Boil the eggs: put the eggs in a pot and fill the pot with cold water until they are completely covered. Place on stove over high heat and bring the water to a boil. Once boiling, reduce the heat to low and simmer for 12 minutes. Remove from heat, drain the water and allow to cool.
2. Blanch green beans: fill a pot with water and bring to a boil over high heat. Once boiling, add the green beans and reduce the heat to low, and simmer for 2 minutes. Remove the beans from the heat and drain. Immediately transfer the beans to a bowl of ice water and let them cool.
3. Rinse and chop the lettuce and bell peppers and place in a large bowl. Add tomatoes, olives, cooled green beans and cooled boiled eggs.
4. Drain the tuna and add it to the salad.
5. In a separate bowl, whisk together the olive oil, white wine vinegar, salt and freshly cracked black pepper.
6. Pour the dressing over the salad and toss to combine.

Nutrition information:
1 serving: 323 Calories; 20.2g Fat; 11.2g Carbs; 24.8g Protein.

57. Ratatouille Provençale

Ratatouille Provençale is a traditional French stew made with vegetables that can be served as a main dish or side dish.
Serving: 4

Preparation time: 15 minutes
Ready time: 40 minutes

Ingredients:
1 b eggplant, 1 large onion, 2 cloves garlic, 1 red bell pepper, 2 zucchini, 1 can (14.5 ounces) diced tomatoes, 1 tablespoon fresh thyme leaves, 2 tablespoons olive oil, Salt and pepper to taste

Instructions:
1. Preheat oven to 375 degrees F.
2. Cut Eggplant, onion, garlic, bell pepper and zucchini into small cubes
3. Transfer to a large bowl and mix with diced tomatoes and thyme leaves
4. Place in a greased baking dish and drizzle with olive oil
5. Bake for 30 minutes, stirring once during baking time
6. Remove from oven, season with salt and pepper and serve

Nutrition information: (per serving) 169 calories, 12g fat, 11g carbohydrates, 7g protein

58. Bouillabaisse à la Marseillaise

Bouillabaisse à la Marseillaise is a traditional seafood and fish stew from Marseille, France. It is a rich and flavorful dish that has Mediterranean influences, making it an incredibly delicious and healthy choice.
Serving: 4 - 6
Preparation Time: 30 minutes
Ready Time: 1 hour 30 minutes

Ingredients:
• 2 tablespoons olive oil
• 1 small onion, chopped
• 1 red bell pepper, chopped
• 6 cups fish stock
• 2 cloves garlic, minced
• 2 medium tomatoes, chopped
• 1 teaspoon dried thyme
• 1 bay leaf
• 1 teaspoon saffron threads

- 2 tablespoons freshly-chopped parsley
- 2 pounds of mixed seafood such as cod, halibut, mussels, clams, scallops, etc.
- Salt and pepper, to taste
- ½ cup of white wine

Instructions:
1. Heat the olive oil in a large pot over medium heat. Add the onion and bell pepper, and cook for 5 minutes, stirring occasionally.
2. Add the fish stock, garlic, tomatoes, thyme, bay leaf, saffron, and parsley. Stir to combine, and bring the mixture to a boil.
3. Reduce the heat to low, and simmer for 20 minutes.
4. Add the mixed seafood and season with salt and pepper. Simmer for 10 minutes.
5. Pour in the white wine and continue to simmer for 10 minutes.
6. Serve the stew with crusty bread.

Nutrition information: per serving: 254 calories; 11.2g fat; 21g protein; 8.4g carbohydrates; 2.4g fiber.

59. Poulet Vallée d'Auge

Poulet Vallée d'Auge is a popular and classic French dish made of chicken with apples and cream. It's a very flavorful and delicious treat that's sure to impress.
Serving: 4
Preparation time: 15 minutes
Ready time: 1 hour

Ingredients:
- 4 chicken thighs
- 2 tablespoons olive oil
- 1 teaspoon salt
- 1 teaspoon black pepper
- 2 onions, diced
- 2 cloves garlic, minced
- 1 teaspoon dried thyme
- 1 teaspoon dried rosemary
- 2 tart apples, cored and cubed

- 2 tablespoons Calvados or cognac
- 1 cup dry white wine
- 1 cup chicken stock
- 1/2 cup heavy cream

Instructions:
1. Preheat oven to 350 degrees F.
2. Heat olive oil in a heavy skillet over medium-high heat.
3. Season chicken with salt and pepper. Add chicken to the skillet and cook for about 5 minutes per side, until lightly browned. Remove from skillet and set aside.
4. Add onions, garlic, thyme, and rosemary to the skillet and cook for 3 minutes, stirring frequently.
5. Add apples to the skillet and cook for 2 minutes.
6. Add the Calvados or cognac to the skillet and bring to a simmer. Simmer for 2 minutes.
7. Add the white wine and reduce by half.
8. Add chicken stock to the skillet and bring to a simmer. Simmer for 15 minutes.
9. Add the chicken to the skillet and return to a simmer.
10. Place the skillet in the preheated oven and bake for 25 minutes.
11. Remove the skillet from the oven and add the cream. Simmer for 5 minutes, stirring occasionally.

Nutrition information:
Calories: 254; Fat: 13g; Protein: 21g; Carbohydrates: 13g; Fiber: 1g; Cholesterol: 85mg; Sodium: 511mg.

60. Tarte au Citron

Tarte au Citron is a classic French lemon tart, featuring a buttery crust and a creamy tart filling made with fresh lemon juice and zest. Its sweet and tart flavor makes it the perfect dessert to enjoy any time.
Serving: 8
Preparation Time: 15 minutes
Ready Time: 45 minutes

Ingredients:

-1 1/2 cups all-purpose flour
-3 tablespoons granulated sugar
-1/2 cup (1 stick) cold butter, cut into pieces
-1 large egg yolk
-Zest of 1 lemon
-2 tablespoons cold water
Filling:
-1/2 cup freshly squeezed lemon juice
-1/3 cup granulated sugar
-3 large eggs
-2 egg yolks
-1/4 cup (1/2 stick) butter
-Pinch of salt

Instructions:
1. For the crust: Preheat the oven to 375°F. Place the flour, sugar, butter, egg yolk, lemon zest and cold water in a food processor. Pulse until the mixture forms small crumbs.
2. Press the dough into a 9-inch tart pan. Prick the bottom with a fork and bake for 15 minutes, or until golden brown.
3. For the filling: In a medium bowl, mix together the lemon juice, sugar, eggs, egg yolks, butter and salt.
4. Pour the filling mixture into the prepared tart shell.
5. Bake for 30 minutes, or until set. Let cool completely.

Nutrition information: Per serving: Calories: 224, Total Fat: 12g, Saturated Fat: 6g, Cholesterol: 82mg, Sodium: 83mg, Carbohydrates: 24g, Fiber: 1g, Sugar: 7g, Protein: 5g

61. Coq au Vin Jaune

Coq au Vin Jaune is a classic French dish that is truly mouthwatering. This hearty stew is full of robust flavors and is made with chicken, onions, mushrooms, and a unique combination of white wine and crème fraîche.
Serving: 4-6
Preparation Time: 20 minutes
Ready Time: 2 hours

Ingredients:
- 2 tablespoons vegetable oil
- 2 1/2 pounds bone-in chicken pieces, such as breasts, thighs, and legs
- 2 small onions, thinly sliced
- 3 cloves garlic, minced
- 1 teaspoon fresh thyme leaves
- 2 cups dry white wine
- 2 cups chicken stock
- 1/2 cup crème fraîche
- 8 ounces mushrooms, sliced
- 2 tablespoons butter
- 2 tablespoons all-purpose flour
- Salt and freshly ground black pepper
- 2 tablespoons chopped fresh parsley

Instructions:
1. Heat the oil in a large saucepan set over medium heat.
2. Add the chicken to the pan and cook for 6 to 8 minutes per side, or until lightly browned.
3. Add the onions, garlic, and thyme to the pan and cook for 3 minutes, or until the onions are softened.
4. Add the wine and stock to the pan and bring the mixture to a boil. Reduce the heat to low and simmer for 30 minutes, or until the chicken is cooked through.
5. Remove the chicken pieces from the pan and set aside.
6. Whisk together the crème fraîche and mushrooms in a small bowl.
7. Increase the heat to medium-high and add the crème fraîche mixture to the pan. Simmer for 10 minutes, or until the sauce is thickened.
8. Return the chicken to the pan and simmer for 5 minutes, or until the chicken is heated through.
9. In a small saucepan, melt the butter over medium-high heat.
10. Whisk in the flour and cook for 1 minute, or until lightly browned.
11. Add the mixture to the pan and cook for 1 minute, or until thickened.
12. Serve the stew immediately with fresh parsley, salt, and pepper to taste.

Nutrition information:

Calories: 375 kcal, Carbohydrates: 9.2 g, Protein: 27.1 g, Fat: 22.1 g, Saturated Fat: 8.5 g, Cholesterol: 107 mg, Sodium: 292 mg, Potassium: 526 mg, Fiber: 1.2 g, Sugar: 2.6 g, Vitamin A: 310 IU, Vitamin C: 7.9 mg, Calcium: 45 mg, Iron: 2.2 mg

62. Tartiflette

Tartiflette is a classic French dish from the Savoy region of France. It is prepared with potatoes, bacon, and cheese and topped with an intoxicating cream sauce. It's sure to please even the pickiest of eaters.
Serving: 4-6
Preparation Time: 10 minutes
Ready Time: 40 minutes

Ingredients:
- 2 lbs potatoes, peeled and diced
- 6 slices bacon, diced
- 1 onion, diced
- 6 ounces Gruyere cheese, shredded
- 1 cup heavy cream
- 2 teaspoons Dijon mustard
- Salt & pepper, to taste

Instructions:
1. Preheat oven to 375 degrees F.
2. In a large pot, boil potatoes until tender, about 15 minutes. Drain and set aside.
3. Cook bacon in a large skillet over medium heat until crisp. Add onion and cook until softened.
4. In a large bowl, mix together cooked potatoes, bacon mixture, and shredded cheese.
5. In a small bowl, whisk together cream and mustard until combined. Pour over potato mixture and mix until everything is evenly coated.
6. Transfer mixture to an oven-safe baking dish.
7. Bake for 25 minutes, or until cheese is melted and bubbling.
8. Serve and enjoy!

Nutrition information: Serving size: 1/6 of recipe | Calories: 452 kcal | Carbohydrates: 32g | Protein: 11g | Fat: 30g | Cholesterol: 83mg | Sodium: 343mg | Potassium: 516mg | Fiber: 3g | Sugar: 2g | Vitamin A: 473IU | Vitamin C: 18mg | Calcium: 199mg | Iron: 1mg

63. Soupe de Poisson

originally hailing from the south of France near Marseille, Soupe de Poisson is a classic French fish soup loaded with hearty vegetables, savory fish, and flavorful herbs.
Serving: 4
Preparation time: 20 minutes
Ready time: 50 minutes

Ingredients:
- 4 tablespoons of olive oil
- 1 large onion, diced
- 1 large carrot, peeled and diced
- 2 celery stalks, diced
- 1 fennel bulb (optional), diced
- 4 cloves of garlic, minced
- 2 tablespoons of tomato paste
- 8 to 12 ounces of white fish filets, cut into 1-inch cubes
- 2 sprigs of fresh thyme
- 2 sprigs of fresh rosemary
- 2 bay leaves
- 1/2 cup of white wine
- 2 cups of vegetable broth
- 2 cups of water
- 2 small potatoes, peeled and cut into 1-inch cubes
- 2 tablespoons of flat-leaf parsley, minced
- Salt and freshly ground pepper, to taste

Instructions:
1. Heat the olive oil in a large pot over medium heat.
2. Add the onion, carrot, celery, and fennel (if using), and cook, stirring occasionally, until the vegetables are tender, about 5 minutes.

3. Add the garlic and tomato paste and cook for 1 minute.
4. Add the fish, thyme, rosemary, bay leaves, wine, vegetable broth, and water. Simmer for 10 minutes.
5. Add the potatoes and cook for an additional 10 minutes.
6. Discard the bay leaves and rosemary. Add the parsley. Season with salt and pepper, to taste.
7. Serve immediately.

Nutrition information: Nutritional information for one serving of Soupe de Poisson (without potatoes): 138 calories, 6.5g fat, 12.7g protein, 2.1g carbohydrates, 0.8g fiber.

64. Côte de Boeuf

Côte de Boeuf is a classic French beef dish, made with a flavorful cut of meat cooked to perfection. Served best with red wine and accompanied by a simple yet tasty sauce, this dish is sure to impress dinner guests.
Serving: 4 servings
Preparation time: 15 minutes
Ready time: 1 hour 20 minutes

Ingredients:
• 4 center cut boneless beef ribeye steaks (2 to 2 ½ lbs)
• 1 ½ teaspoons kosher salt
• 1 teaspoon freshly ground black pepper
• 2 Tablespoons olive oil
• 1 large onion, finely diced
• 4 cloves garlic, minced
• 2 cups beef broth
• 1 cup red wine
• 2 teaspoons fresh thyme leaves
• 2 Tablespoons tomato paste
• 2 Tablespoons butter
• 2 Tablespoons all-purpose flour

Instructions:
1. Preheat the oven to 350°F.
2. Season the steaks with 1 teaspoon salt and 1/2 teaspoon pepper. Heat the olive oil in a large oven-safe skillet over medium-high heat.

3. When the oil is hot, add the steaks to the skillet and cook for 4 minutes per side. Transfer the steaks to a plate and set aside.
4. To the same skillet, add the onion and cook for 5 minutes, stirring occasionally until the onion is softened. Add garlic and cook until fragrant, about one minute.
5. Add the beef broth, red wine, thyme, and tomato paste. Bring to a simmer, scraping up any browned bits. Simmer for 7 minutes.
6. Return the steaks to the skillet. Cover and place in the oven for 30 minutes.
7. While the steaks are cooking, melt the butter in a small saucepan over medium heat. Whisk in the flour and cook for 2 minutes.
8. Slowly whisk in the pan juices from the steaks. Simmer for 10 minutes, whisking until thickened.
9. Remove the steaks from the oven and transfer to a serving plate. Cover with foil to keep warm.
10. Serve the steaks with the sauce. Enjoy!

Nutrition information: Calories: 590, Total Fat: 41 g, Saturated Fat: 18 g, Cholesterol: 155 mg, Sodium: 650 mg, Carbohydrates: 7 g, Fiber: 1 g, Sugar: 2 g, Protein: 49 g

65. Tarte Tropézienne

The Tarte Tropézienne is a traditional French cake that originated in Saint-Tropez in the 1950s. It is an almond and orange blossom flavored round cake, filled with a creamy custard-like center and topped with a sugar glaze.
Serving: 8-10
Preparation time: 55 minutes
Ready time: 1 hour 15 minutes

Ingredients:
• 5 large eggs, separated
• 2/3 cup granulated sugar plus 1/4 cup for meringue
• 2 tablespoons all-purpose flour
• 3 tablespoons almond meal
• 2 tablespoons orange blossom water
• 2/3 cup butter, softened
• 1/2 teaspoon vanilla extract

- 2 tablespoons confectioners' sugar
- 2 tablespoons heavy cream

Instructions:
1. Preheat the oven to 350°F.
2. Beat the egg whites in a medium bowl with an electric mixer until soft peaks form. Add 1/4 cup of sugar gradually, and continue beating until stiff peaks form. Set aside.
3. In a separate bowl, beat the egg yolks and the remaining 2/3 cup of sugar until light and fluffy.
4. Add the butter, almond meal, flour, vanilla extract and orange blossom water, and beat until combined.
5. Gently fold in the egg whites.
6. Grease an 8-inch spring form pan, and spread the batter in it.
7. Bake for 35-40 minutes, or until golden brown.
8. Let cool completely.
9. Using a hand mixer, beat the cream and confectioners' sugar until light and fluffy.
10. Spread the cream over the cake, and serve.

Nutrition information:
Per Serving: Calories: 310 Total Fat: 16g Saturated Fat: 10g Cholesterol: 101mg Sodium: 89mg Carbohydrate: 33g Fiber: 1g Sugars: 18g Protein: 6g Vitamin A: 629IU Vitamin C: 0mg Calcium: 70mg Iron: 1mg

66. Pâté de Campagne

Pâté de Campagne, a rustic and earthy French terrine, is a delicious combination of pork, liver, vegetables, and spices, all bind together and cooked slowly in the oven.
Serving: 6-8
Preparation Time: 45 mins
Ready Time: 2 hours 20 mins

Ingredients:
-1 lb pork shoulder, roughly chopped
-7 oz diced pork liver
-3 cloves garlic, chopped

-2 medium-sized onions, chopped
-2 carrots, chopped
-2 celery stalks, chopped
-2 tablespoons butter
-2 tablespoons cognac
-1 teaspoon fresh thyme
-1 bay leaf
-1 teaspoon freshly cracked pepper
-3 tablespoons all-purpose flour
-1 teaspoon freshly squeezed lemon juice
-1/2 cup heavy cream
-Salt, to taste

Instructions:
1. Begin by preheating the oven to 350°F.
2. In a large mixing bowl, combine the pork, liver, garlic, onions, carrots, celery, butter, cognac, thyme, bay leaf, pepper, flour, and lemon juice. With clean hands, mix the Ingredients together until well combined.
3. Grease a 9-inch loaf pan and line with foil. Pour the mixture into the pan and spread it out evenly.
4. Bake in the preheated oven for 1 hour and 10 minutes.
5. Remove the pan from the oven and pour the cream over the top evenly. Bake for an additional 10 minutes.
6. Remove from the oven and let cool. Remove the pâté from the pan and slice into pieces.

Nutrition information:
Calories: 268; Protein: 15.4g; Fat: 15.9g; Carbohydrates: 12.1g; Sugar: 2.8g; Fiber: 1.6g; Sodium: 516.2mg.

67. Salade Lyonnaise

Salade Lyonnaise is a classic French dish based on a simple salad. It is typically made with frisée lettuce, lardons or diced bacon, a poached egg, and croutons. This delicious salad is a popular culinary tradition in Lyon, the third largest city in France.
Serving: 4
Preparation Time: 15 minutes

Ready Time: 20 minutes

Ingredients:
- 9 ounces frisée lettuce
- 4 ounces bacon, diced
- 4 large eggs
- 2 tablespoons unsalted butter
- 2 tablespoons extra-virgin olive oil
- 2 tablespoons white wine vinegar
- 1 garlic clove, minced
- Salt and freshly ground black pepper
- 1 French-style baguette, sliced and toasted
- Optional: 1 hard boiled egg, diced

Instructions:
1. Place the diced bacon in a large skillet over medium-high heat and cook for 8-10 minutes, or until crisp. Remove the bacon from the pan and set aside.
2. In the same pan, add the butter and olive oil and heat for 1 minute. Add the minced garlic and cook for an additional 30 seconds.
3. Add the white wine vinegar to the pan and simmer for 2 minutes.
4. Place the frisée lettuce in a large bowl and pour the bacon and garlic dressing over top.
5. Slice the baguette and toast for 4-5 minutes or until lightly golden.
6. In a separate skillet, bring a pot of water to a simmer and carefully crack each egg into the water. Poach for approximately 3 minutes, or until the yolks are just set and the whites are tender.
7. Assemble the salad by placing the frisée lettuce on each plate. Top each salad with the bacon, poached eggs, optional diced hard boiled egg, and toasted baguette slices.
8. Drizzle the remaining bacon and garlic dressing over the salads and season with salt and pepper to taste.

Nutrition information:
Calories: 345, Fat: 13 g, Carbohydrates: 34 g, Protein: 18 g, Sodium: 676 mg

68. Pissaladière Niçoise

Pissaladière Niçoise is a pizza-like pastry popular in the southeastern region of France. It is topped with caramelized onions, anchovies, and olives and is one of the most deliciously savory dishes of Provençal cuisine.

Serving: 4
Preparation Time: 15 minutes
Ready Time: 45 minutes

Ingredients:
- 2 tablespoons of extra virgin olive oil
- 1 large onion, thinly sliced
- Salt and pepper to taste
- 2 anchovy fillets, chopped
- 1 can of black olives, pitted and chopped
- 2 cloves of garlic, minced
- 2 tablespoons of fresh thyme
- 2 tablespoons of fresh oregano
- 1 sheet of puff pastry
- 2 tablespoons of grated Parmesan cheese

Instructions:
1. Preheat the oven to 375°F.
2. Heat the olive oil in a large skillet over medium-high heat. Add the onions and season with salt and pepper. Cook, stirring occasionally, until lightly browned, about 10 minutes.
3. Add the anchovies, olives, garlic, thyme, and oregano, and cook, stirring occasionally, for an additional 5 minutes.
4. Transfer the mixture onto a parchment-lined baking sheet and spread it out evenly.
5. Place the puff pastry sheet over the mixture and crimp the edges. Sprinkle the Parmesan cheese on top and bake for 25 minutes.
6. Remove from the oven and let cool for 5 minutes before slicing and serving.

Nutrition information:
Calories: 225, Fat: 12.5 g, Cholesterol: 0 mg, Sodium: 276 mg, Carbohydrates: 20 g, Protein: 7.5 g

69. Crème Brûlée

Crème Brûlée is a classic French dessert and translates to "burnt cream". It consists of a creamy custard base topped with a crunchy layer of caramelized sugar.

Serving: 6
Preparation Time: 15 minutes
Ready Time: 1 hour

Ingredients:
- 3 cups heavy cream
- 1/4 cup granulated white sugar
- 5 large egg yolks
- 1 teaspoon vanilla extract
- 6 tablespoons granulated white sugar for topping

Instructions:
1. Preheat the oven to 350F degrees.
2. In a medium saucepan, heat cream and 1/4 cup sugar just until it starts to simmer.
3. Meanwhile, in a medium bowl, whisk the egg yolks and remaining sugar until creamy.
4. Slowly add the heated cream mixture and blend well.
5. Add the vanilla extract and mix until combined.
6. Take six 6-ounce ramekins and divide the custard mixture evenly among them.
7. Put the ramekins in a baking dish and add hot water up to the middle of the ramekin.
8. Bake for approximately 30-35 minutes until the custards are set.
9. Place the ramekins on a wire rack and cool to room temperature.
10. Once cool, sprinkle the sugar over the top of each custard and brulee with a kitchen torch or under the broiler for about 2 minutes until the sugar melts and caramelizes.

Nutrition information:
Total Calories: 549, Fat: 37.2g, Carbs: 42.4g, Protein: 6.1g

70. Cassoulet Toulousain

Cassoulet Toulousain is a rustic, hearty French dish, traditionally made with white beans, meat and vegetables. It is often cooked in a heavy clay or ceramic pot.

Serving: Serves 4-6
Preparation time: 15 minutes
Ready time: 1 hour 15 minutes

Ingredients:

- 2 tablespoons olive oil
- 2 onions, diced
- 2 cloves garlic, minced
- 500g pork shoulder, diced
- 1 teaspoon dried thyme
- 2 tablespoons tomato paste
- 4 cups chicken stock
- 2 cans cannellini beans, drained and rinsed
- 2 smoked duck legs
- 2 smoked pork sausages
- 2 bay leaves
- 2 tablespoons parsley, chopped

Instructions:

1. Preheat oven to 160°C.
2. Heat the oil in a large oven-safe pot over medium heat, and sauté the onions and garlic until softened.
3. Add the pork and thyme and cook until the pork is slightly browned.
4. Add the tomato paste and stir through.
5. Pour in the chicken stock and bring to a simmer.
6. Add the cannellini beans, duck legs, sausages and bay leaves and give everything a good stir.
7. Cover and place in the oven for 1 hour.
8. Remove from the oven, add the parsley and season to taste with salt and pepper.

Nutrition information: Calories: 425, Fat: 17.4g, Saturated fat: 4.7g, Carbohydrates: 32.8g, Sugar: 5.3g, Protein: 28.8g, Sodium: 739mg, Fiber: 12.1g.

71. Quiche au Saumon

Quiche au Saumon is a delicious French quiche recipe that features smoked salmon, fresh dill, and a cheesy custard for a flavorful, savory entree that is sure to impress.

Serving:
Serves 8
Preparation time: 25 minutes
Ready time: 1 hour

Ingredients:
- 1 9- or 10-inch pre-baked pastry shell, defrosted if frozen
- 4 cups cubed, cooked potatoes
- 12 ounces smoked salmon, cut into small cubes
- 1/2 cup chopped fresh dill
- 4 large eggs
- 1/2 cup half-and-half
- 1 cup grated Gruyere cheese
- Salt and pepper, to taste

Instructions:
1. Preheat the oven to 350°F.
2. Spread the potatoes and smoked salmon in the pastry shell. Sprinkle with the chopped dill.
3. In a medium bowl, whisk together the eggs, half-and-half, Gruyere cheese, salt and pepper until combined.
4. Pour the cheese mixture over the potatoes, smoked salmon, and dill in the pastry shell.
5. Bake the quiche in the preheated oven for 35 to 40 minutes until it's golden and set.
6. Cool the quiche for 15 to 20 minutes before serving, and enjoy!

Nutrition information:
Calories: 373Kcal, Protein: 16g, Fat: 22g, Carbohydrates: 25g, Sugar: 3g, Sodium: 316mg, Fiber: 2g

72. Canard à l'Orange

Canard à l'Orange is a classic French dish that is made with duck and an orange-based sauce. This decadent dish is both sweet and savory and perfect for a special occasion.

Serving: 6

Preparation Time: 15 minutes

Ready Time: 1 hour 20 minutes

Ingredients:

-2 duck legs
-1 teaspoon of ground sea salt
-1 teaspoon of ground black pepper
-1 large orange
-¼ cup of raisins
-¼ cup of diced shallots
-2 tablespoons of olive oil
-2 cloves of garlic, minced
-1 cup of port wine
-½ cup of orange juice
-2 tablespoons of honey
-2 tablespoons of balsamic vinegar

Instructions:

1. Preheat oven to 350°F (175°C).
2. Place the duck legs in an oven-safe container and season with salt and black pepper.
3. Slice the orange into wedges and add to the container.
4. Add the raisins, shallots, olive oil, garlic, port wine, orange juice, honey, and balsamic vinegar to the container and stir everything together.
5. Place the container in the preheated oven and bake for 1 hour.
6. Remove from oven and serve.

Nutrition information:

Calories: 500

Fat: 34g

Carbohydrates: 39g

Protein: 22g

73. Truite Meunière

Truite Meunière is a classic French fish dish featuring pan-fried trout coated with brown butter, fresh parsley and lemon wedges. It is simple to make and makes for a delicious and healthy meal.

Serving: 2
Preparation Time: 10 minutes
Ready Time: 15 minutes

Ingredients:
2 trout fillets
2 tablespoons butter
1 tablespoon olive oil
Salt & pepper
2 tablespoons chopped flat-leaf parsley
2 lemon wedges

Instructions:
1. Heat the butter and olive oil in a skillet over medium-high heat.
2. Once the butter is hot and bubbly, season the trout fillets with salt and pepper and place them in the pan skin side down.
3. Cook the trout for 4-5 minutes, or until it is lightly browned. Flip the trout over and cook for an additional 4-5 minutes.
4. Once the trout is cooked through, remove it from the pan and transfer to a serving plate.
5. Add the butter to the skillet and cook it until it turns golden-brown and begins to bubble.
6. Pour the browned butter over the trout and garnish with the chopped parsley and lemon wedges.

Nutrition information: One serving of Truite Meunière provides 182 calories, 10.9 grams of fat, 2.4 grams of saturated fat, 5.2 grams of carbohydrates, 0.7 gram of fiber, 0.2 gram of sugar, and 19.7 grams of protein.

74. Navarin d'Agneau

Navarin d'Agneau is a traditional French stew made with succulent pieces of spring lamb, white onions and baby vegetables. It's a comforting and flavorful classic that's perfect for the whole family to enjoy.

Serving: 6

Preparation Time: 10 minutes

Ready time: 40 minutes

Ingredients:

- 2 tablespoons olive oil
- 2lbs boneless spring lamb, cubed
- 3 cups cold water
- 2 onions, chopped
- 4 large carrots, peeled and cut into 2-inch pieces
- 2 celery stalks, cut into 2-inch pieces
- 1/2 cup fresh or frozen green peas
- 4 small waxy potatoes, cut into 1-inch cubes
- 2 cloves garlic, minced
- 2 tablespoons tomato paste
- 2 tablespoons fresh parsley, chopped
- 2 teaspoons fresh thyme leaves
- 1 bay leaf
- Salt and ground pepper

Instructions:

1. Heat the oil in a large pot over medium heat. Add the diced lamb and cook until lightly browned, about 5 minutes, stirring occasionally.

2. Add the onions, carrots, celery and potatoes to the pot. Cook for 5 minutes, stirring occasionally.

3. Stir in the garlic, tomato paste, parsley, thyme and bay leaf. Season with salt and pepper. Add the cold water, bring to a simmer and cook for 10 minutes.

4. Reduce the heat to low, cover with a lid and simmer until the lamb is tender, about 25 minutes. Add the green peas during the last 5 minutes of cooking.

5. Serve the navarin d'agneau with boiled or mashed potatoes.

Nutrition information: Per Serving: Calories 352; Fat 18g (Saturated 4g); Cholesterol 99mg; Sodium 282mg; Carbohydrate 17g; Fiber 5g; Protein 28g

75. Escalope de Veau

Escalope de Veau is a French dish that is made from thin slices of veal known as escalopes. This dish is often cooked in a white wine sauce with mushrooms, onions, and garlic, lending it a delicious flavor.
Serving: Serves 4
Preparation Time: 15 minutes
Ready Time: 45 minutes

Ingredients:
- 4 veal escalopes
- 3 onions, finely chopped
- 2 cloves garlic, minced
- 2 tablespoons vegetable oil
- 1/2 cup white wine
- 8 ounces button mushrooms, quartered
- 2 tablespoons butter
- Salt and pepper, to taste

Instructions:
1. Heat the oil in a large skillet over medium heat.
2. Add the onions and garlic and sauté until the onions are softened and beginning to brown, about 8 minutes.
3. Remove the onions and garlic from the skillet and set aside.
4. Season the escalopes with salt and pepper and add them to the skillet. Cook until golden brown, about 3 minutes per side.
5. Add the white wine, mushrooms, butter, and the reserved onions and garlic to the skillet. Stir to combine, reduce the heat to low, and simmer until the sauce is thickened and the mushrooms are cooked through, about 20 minutes.
6. Serve the escalopes with the sauce.

Nutrition information:
Calories: 205, Fat: 11.2g, Saturated fat: 4.7g, Carbohydrates: 4.7g, Protein: 17.7g, Sodium: 191mg.

76. Pithiviers

Pithiviers is a classic French pastry, made with an almond cream filling and puff pastry. It makes an impressive dessert and is perfect for special occasions!
Serving: 8
Preparation Time: 40 minutes
Ready Time: 1 hour

Ingredients:
- 500g Puff Pastry
- 125g Ground Almonds
- 125g Caster Sugar
- 140g Butter
- 2 Eggs
- 2 tsp Almond Extract
- 2 tbsp Apricot Jam
- 1 Egg Yolk, beaten

Instructions:
1. Preheat oven to 400°F/200°C.
2. Roll out the puff pastry and put in a 20cm greased tart tin.
3. Put the ground almonds, caster sugar, butter, eggs, almond extract, and apricot jam into a bowl and mix until well blended.
4. Spoon the filling onto the puff pastry and spread it out evenly.
5. Fold up the edges of the pastry and brush with the egg yolk.
6. Bake in the preheated oven for 35-40 minutes, or until golden brown.
7. Serve warm.

Nutrition information (per serving): Calories: 411, Fat: 22.5g, Protein: 6.3g, Carbs: 40.9g, Sugar: 11.2g, Sodium: 144.7mg.

77. Côtelettes d'Agneau

Côtelettes d'Agneau is a French dish made with lamb chops and aromatic herbs. It is an easy and tasty meal that can be served as part of a formal dinner or as a casual weekday dinner.
Serving: Serves 4
Preparation Time: 10 minutes
Ready Time: 1 hour

Ingredients:
- 4 lamb chops
- 2 tablespoons olive oil
- 2 sprigs fresh rosemary
- 2 cloves garlic, chopped
- Sea salt
- Freshly ground black pepper

Instructions:
1. Preheat oven to 375 degrees F (190 degrees Celsius). Pat lamb chops dry and place on a baking sheet.
2. Drizzle with olive oil, then sprinkle with rosemary, garlic, salt and pepper.
3. Bake for 25-30 minutes or until internal temperature of the lamb chops registers at least 165 degrees F (74 degrees Celsius).
4. Serve with desired side dishes.

Nutrition information: Calories -326, Fat - 21.3g, Protein -33.7g, Carbohydrates - 0g, Sodium- 192mg

78. Salade de Chèvre Chaud

Salade de Chèvre Chaud is a warm salad dish prepared with goat cheese. Its sweet and savory taste makes it a great side dish for dinner.
Serving: 4
Preparation Time: 10 Minutes
Ready Time: 20 Minutes

Ingredients:
- 4 ounces goat cheese
- 2 tablespoons butter
- 2 tablespoons olive oil
- 8 ounces arugula
- 4 tablespoons walnuts
- Salt and pepper to taste

Instructions:
1. Preheat oven to 350°F.

2. Place butter in a small baking dish and set in preheated oven until butter is melted.
3. Remove from oven and keep warm.
4. Drizzle goat cheese with melted butter and set aside.
5. Heat olive oil in a large skillet over medium heat.
6. Add the arugula and walnuts to the skillet and season with salt and pepper.
7. Cook, stirring occasionally, until arugula is wilted, about 3 minutes.
8. Divide the arugula mixture among four plates and top each with a piece of the goat cheese.
9. Serve immediately.

Nutrition information:
Calories: 221, Total Fat: 18 grams, Saturated Fat: 5.7 grams, Cholesterol: 16 milligrams, Sodium: 139 milligrams, Carbohydrates: 6.6 grams, Dietary Fiber: 1.7 grams, Sugar: 1.7 grams, Protein: 9.7 grams.

79. Confit de Canard avec Pommes Sarladaises

Confit de Canard avec Pommes Sarladaises is a traditional duck and potato dish from the South West of France. It is a classic that dates back to the Middle Ages and is still popular today. It consists of slow-cooked duck that is served with potatoes cooked in duck fat and garlic.
Serving: 4
Preparation time: 30 minutes
Ready time: 4 hours

Ingredients:
- 4 duck legs
- 3 tablespoons of sea salt
- 2 tablespoons of thyme
- 2 bay leaves
- ½ teaspoon of ground black pepper
- 2 pounds of large Yukon gold potatoes
- 5 tablespoons of duck fat
- 5 cloves of garlic

Instructions:

1. Preheat the oven to 225 degrees Fahrenheit.
2. Rinse the duck legs and pat them dry.
3. Mix together the sea salt, thyme, bay leaves, and black pepper and sprinkle this over the duck legs.
4. Place the duck legs in an oven-safe casserole dish along with the duck fat.
5. Cook the duck legs in the oven for 4 hours, turning them every hour.
6. After 4 hours, remove the duck from the oven and set aside.
7. Peel and cut the potatoes into thick slices and place them into the duck fat from the casserole.
8. Add the garlic cloves and stir gently.
9. Place the casserole back into the oven and cook for an additional 30 minutes until the potatoes are golden and crispy.
10. Serve the potatoes with the duck legs and enjoy!
Nutrition information: Per Serving: 467 calories, 29g fat, 28g carbohydrates, 28g protein.

80. Choucroute Garnie

Choucroute Garnie is a traditional dish from the Alsace region of France. It is a simple, delicious dish made from sauerkraut, various types of smoked meat, potatoes, and onions.
Serving: Serves 4
Preparation time: 5 minutes
Ready time: 2 hours

Ingredients:
- 2 teaspoons of extra virgin olive oil
- 4 onions, finely sliced
- 5-6 cloves garlic, chopped
- 4 medium potatoes, peeled and quartered
- 2 pounds of sauerkraut, drained and rinsed
- 2 cups of white wine
- 2 bay leaves
- 2 cups of water
- 8 ounces of smoked bacon lardons
- 12 ounces of smoked sausage, cut into bite-sized pieces
- 4 ounces of smoked ham, finely cubed

- 2 tablespoons caraway seeds

Instructions:
1. Heat the olive oil in a large pot over medium heat.
2. Add the onions and garlic and cook until the onions are softened, about 8 minutes.
3. Add the potatoes, sauerkraut, white wine, bay leaves, and water. Bring to a simmer.
4. Add the bacon, sausage, and ham.
5. Simmer for 1 hour, stirring occasionally.
6. Add the caraway seeds and simmer for an additional 30 minutes.
7. Serve hot with a loaf of crusty bread.

Nutrition information: Calories: 515g, Carbohydrates: 44g, Protein: 15g, Fat: 30g, Sodium: 1517mg, Sugar: 11g.

81. Coquilles Saint-Jacques Gratinées

Coquilles Saint-Jacques Gratinées, also known as scallops gratin, is a classic French seafood offering. The scallops are topped with cheese and herbs, and then baked to create a creamy, flavorful entrée.
Serving: 4
Preparation Time: 10 minutes
Ready Time: 25 minutes

Ingredients:
• 8 large scallops
• 2 ounces of grated cheese (Gruyere or Swiss)
• 2 tablespoons butter, melted
• 2 tablespoons dry white wine
• 1 tablespoon chopped fresh parsley or chives
• Salt and pepper to taste

Instructions:
1. Preheat oven to 375 degrees F (190 degrees C).
2. Place scallops in a lightly greased baking dish.
3. Sprinkle the cheese over the scallops.
4. In a small bowl, combine 1 tablespoon of the melted butter, wine, parsley or chives, salt and pepper; stir to mix.

5. Drizzle this mixture over the cheese and scallops.
6. Pour the remaining butter over all.
7. Bake for 25 minutes or until the scallops are done to your liking.

Nutrition information:
- Calories: 157
- Total Fat: 10.7g
- Cholesterol: 60.2mg
- Sodium: 249.1mg
- Total Carbohydrates: 1.1g
- Dietary Fiber: 0.1g
- Protein: 12.9g

82. Rillettes de Porc

Rillettes de Porc is a French-style pork pâté, which has a coarse texture and is usually served with toast or crackers. It is a popular dish in many parts of Europe and although often served as an appetizer, it can also be served as a main course.
Serving: 4-6
Preparation time: 15 minutes
Ready time: 1 hour 15 minutes

Ingredients:
- 2 1/2 lb boneless pork shoulder
- 2 tsp coarse salt
- 2 tsp freshly ground pepper
- 5 peeled garlic cloves
- 6 whole cloves
- 2 tsp fresh thyme leaves
- 2 cups unsalted chicken stock
- 2 tbsp white vermouth

Instructions:
1. Cut the pork into 2-inch cubes and season with salt and pepper.
2. Place the garlic, cloves, and thyme into a food processor and finely mince.

3. Heat the chicken stock and vermouth in a large pot over medium-high heat.

4. Add the pork cubes and minced aromatics to the pot and cook, stirring occasionally, for about 45 minutes.

5. When the pork is tender and beginning to break apart, remove from heat and allow to cool slightly.

6. When the pork is cool enough to handle, shred it with two forks until it is finely crumbled.

7. Return the shredded pork to the cooking liquid and allow to simmer over low heat for 30 minutes.

8. Transfer to a shallow dish, allow to cool, and serve.

Nutrition information: 435 calories; 28g fat; 0g carbohydrates; 31g protein.

83. Filet Mignon en Croûte

Filet Mignon en Croûte is a traditional French dish that creates an unforgettable gourmet experience. This recipe calls for fresh Ingredients, making it simple yet elegant.
Serving: 4
Preparation Time: 10 minutes
Ready Time: 50 minutes

Ingredients:
• 4 Filet Mignon steaks
• 4 tablespoons butter
• 2 tablespoons of Dijon mustard
• 2 tablespoons of chopped fresh parsley
• 2 garlic cloves, minced
• Salt & pepper
• 4 ounces bacon
• 2 tablespoons of olive oil
• 4 slices of Swiss cheese
• 4 pieces of puff pastry

Instructions:
1. Preheat the oven to 375°F.
2. In a small bowl, mix together the butter, mustard, parsley and garlic.

3. Season the filet mignon steaks with salt and pepper to your taste.
4. Spread the mustard-butter mixture on each steak and then wrap the steak in bacon.
5. Place the steaks on a baking sheet that has been greased with olive oil.
6. Lay one piece of puff pastry on top of each steak.
7. Place a slice of cheese on top of the puff pastry.
8. Bake the steaks in the preheated oven for 30-40 minutes, or until the puff pastry is golden brown.
9. Let the steaks rest for 10 minutes before serving.

Nutrition information: (Serving size 4 ounces)
- Calories: 287
- Total Fat: 21.5 g
- Cholesterol: 58 mg
- Sodium: 335 mg
- Total Carbohydrates: 4.2 g
- Protein: 16.8 g

84. Quiche de Lorraine

Quiche de Lorraine is a classic French savory tart - an egg and cream custard baked in a tart shell and topped with bacon and cheese for a rich and delicious meal.
Serving: 6-8
Preparation time: 25 minutes
Ready time: 40-45 minutes

Ingredients:
- 1 (9-inch) pre-cooked deep dish tart shell
- 8 ounces bacon, cooked and crumbled
- 1 cup grated Gruyere cheese
- 4 eggs
- 1 cup cream
- 1/4 teaspoon ground nutmeg
- Salt and freshly ground black pepper, to taste

Instructions:
1. Preheat oven to 350°F.

2. Place the pre-cooked tart shell on a baking sheet.

3. Sprinkle the bacon and cheese evenly over the bottom of the tart shell.

4. In a medium bowl, whisk together the eggs, cream, nutmeg, and salt and pepper.

5. Pour the egg mixture over the bacon and cheese in the tart shell.

6. Bake for 40-45 minutes, or until the custard is set.

7. Allow to cool before cutting into slices and serving.

Nutrition information:
Calories: 215, Fat: 16g, Cholesterol: 99mg, Sodium: 366mg, Carbohydrates: 11g, Fiber: 1g, Protein: 9g

85. Salade de Magret de Canard

Salade de Magret de Canard is a delicious French dish made with slices of grilled duck and fresh, seasonal greens. The combination of textures, flavors, and colors of this dish make it a must-try for food lovers!
Serving: 4
Preparation Time: 30 minutes
Ready Time: 30 minutes

Ingredients:
• 4 magret de canard slices
• 2 romaine lettuce heads, thinly sliced
• 2 cups arugula
• 1 cup cherry tomatoes, halved
• 2 radishes, thinly sliced
• 2 tablespoons fresh parsley, finely chopped
• 2 tablespoons olive oil
• 2 teaspoons lemon juice
• Salt and pepper, to taste

Instructions:
1. Preheat a grill or griddle pan.
2. Grill the magret de canard slices for about 4 minutes on each side or until cooked through.
3. Transfer cooked magret to a cutting board and let it rest for at least 5 minutes.

4. Meanwhile, in a large bowl, combine the romaine, arugula, tomatoes, radishes, parsley, olive oil, and lemon juice.
5. Season with salt and pepper, and toss until well combined.
6. Slice the magret into thin strips and add them to the salad.
7. Toss again and serve.

Nutrition information (per serving):
Calories: 266
Fat: 25g
Carbohydrates: 3g
Protein: 10g
Sodium: 274mg

86. Soupe à l'Oignon Gratinee

Soupe à l'Oignon Gratinée is a classic French onion soup made up of beef broth, herbs, and caramelized onions mixed with croutons and topped with melted Gruyère cheese. It is a rich and flavorful soup that is sure to satisfy your taste buds!
Serving: 4-6
Preparation Time: 25 minutes
Ready Time: 1 hour

Ingredients:
- 2 tablespoons olive oil
- 4 large onions, peeled and sliced
- 2 cloves garlic, minced
- 2 tablespoons all-purpose flour
- 6 cups beef broth
- 2 sprigs fresh thyme
- 2 bay leaves
- 2 teaspoons Worcestershire sauce
- 4 tablespoons dry sherry
- Salt and pepper to taste
- 1 French baguette
- 2 cups grated Gruyère cheese

Instructions:
1. Preheat oven to 350 degrees F.

2. Heat oil in a large stock pot over medium-high heat. Add onions and sauté until golden and caramelized, about 8 minutes.
3. Add garlic and sauté an additional 1 minute. Add flour and cook for 2 minutes, stirring periodically.
4. Pour in beef broth, stir in thyme, bay leaves, Worcestershire sauce, sherry, and salt and pepper. Simmer for 10-15 minutes.
5. Slice baguette into 1/2-inch thick slices and lay on a baking sheet. Top each slice with grated cheese. Bake in preheated oven until cheese is melted and lightly browned, about 15 minutes.
6. Pour soup into oven-safe bowls. Place a slice of baguette on top of each bowl and top with melted cheese. Place bowls on a baking sheet and bake in preheated oven until cheese on top is melted and bubbly, about 8-10 minutes.

Nutrition information:
Calories: 382 | Fat: 16g | Protein: 21.4g | Carbs: 34.4g | Fiber: 3.6g

87. Bouillabaisse du Marseillais

Bouillabaisse du Marseillais is a classic French seafood stew, originating from the coastal port city of Marseille. This delicious and nutritious dish combines a variety of fish, shellfish, and potatoes poached slowly in a flavorful broth.
Serving: 8-10
Preparation Time: 30 minutes
Ready Time: 45 minutes

Ingredients:
-2 lbs assorted fresh fish (such as cod, sea bass, monkfish, John Dory, or halibut), cut into 1-inch cubes
-2 lbs shellfish (such as mussels, clams, and prawns), cleaned
-2 large potatoes, peeled and cut into ½-inch cubes
-2 medium onions, diced
-1 medium carrot, peeled and diced
-3 cloves garlic, minced
-2 bay leaves
-4 tbsp olive oil
-4 cups vegetable broth

-2 tbsp tomato paste
-1/4 cup white wine
-1/2 bunch parsley, finely chopped
-2 tsp herbes de Provence
-1/4 tsp red pepper flakes
-Salt and pepper, to taste

Instructions:
1. Heat the olive oil in a large Dutch oven over medium heat.
2. Add the onions, carrots, and garlic and cook, stirring, until the vegetables are softened, about 5 minutes.
3. Add the potatoes, bay leaves, herbes de Provence, and red pepper flakes and cook, stirring, for 2 minutes.
4. Add the vegetable broth, tomato paste, and white wine and bring to a boil. Reduce heat to low and simmer until the potatoes are tender, about 15 minutes.
5. Add the fish and shellfish to the pot and cook for 5 minutes.
6. Add the parsley and season with salt and pepper, to taste.
7. Serve the bouillabaisse with crusty bread and a glass of white wine.

Nutrition information:
Calories: 295, Total Fat: 7g, Cholesterol: 49mg, Sodium: 774mg, Total Carbohydrates: 26g, Dietary Fiber: 4g, Sugars: 7g, Protein: 27g.

88. Oeufs en Meurette

Oeufs en Meurette is a classic French dish originating from the Burgundy region, featuring poached eggs in a red wine and bacon sauce.
Serving: 6
Preparation time: 10 minutes
Ready time: 20 minutes

Ingredients:
- 6 eggs
- 4 ounces bacon, cut into small pieces
- 1 cup red wine
- 1/2 teaspoon Dijon mustard
- 2 tablespoons butter

- 2 tablespoons minced shallots
- 1 tablespoon minced parsley
- Salt and pepper to taste

Instructions:
1. In a large skillet, cook the bacon over medium heat until it is lightly browned.
2. Add the shallots and cook until softened, about 2 minutes.
3. Add the red wine and bring the mixture to a boil. Reduce the heat to low and simmer until the liquid is reduced by half.
4. Add the mustard, butter, parsley, and salt and pepper to taste. Simmer for another 3 minutes, stirring occasionally.
5. Carefully crack the eggs into the skillet and poach until the whites are set, about 3 minutes.
6. Serve the eggs with the sauce drizzled over the top.

Nutrition information:
Calories: 176, Carbs: 0g, Fat:10g, Protein: 7g, Sodium: 163mg, Cholesterol:125mg

89. Ratatouille à la Provençale

Ratatouille à la Provençale is a classic French dish made with seasonal vegetables such as bell pepper, onion, tomato, eggplant, and zucchini in a tomato-based sauce. It packs a punch of flavor with herbs like oregano and thyme, making it a must-try dish!
Serving: 4
Preparation Time: 15 minutes
Ready Time: 45 minutes

Ingredients:
• 2 tablespoons extra-virgin olive oil
• 1 onion, finely chopped
• 2 bell peppers, cut into small cubes
• 2 cloves garlic, minced
• 1 large eggplant, cut into small cubes
• 1 zucchini, cut into small cubes
• 1 (14.5-ounce) can diced tomatoes, well drained
• 1 teaspoon dried oregano

- 1 teaspoon dried thyme
- Salt and freshly ground black pepper, to taste
- 1/4 cup fresh basil, thinly sliced

Instructions:
1. Heat the olive oil in a large skillet over medium heat.
2. Add the onion, bell pepper, garlic, eggplant, and zucchini. Cook until softened, about 10 minutes, stirring occasionally.
3. Add the diced tomatoes, oregano, thyme, salt and pepper. Cook for an additional 15 minutes, stirring occasionally.
4. Add the fresh basil and cook for an additional minute.

Nutrition information: One serving of this Ratatouille à la Provençale provides 98 calories, 4.4g fat, 12.5g carbohydrates, 3.8g protein, 2.4g fiber, and 97mg sodium.

90. Pâté en Croûte

Pâté en Croûte is a classic French dish consisting of a savory pastry filled with steak, veal, pork, or other meats, along with seasonings, spices, and other Ingredients. This dish is the perfect showstopper for any special occasion meal.
Serving: Serves 4-6
Preparation Time: 45 minutes
Ready Time: 2 hours

Ingredients:
-1 package of all-butter puff pastry
-2 tablespoons Dijon mustard
-1 pound coarsely ground pork
-3 tablespoons brandy
-1 teaspoon ground cloves
-1 tablespoon black pepper
-1 teaspoon salt
-1 1/2 tablespoons herbes de Provence
-2 tablespoons egg wash

Instructions:
1. Preheat your oven to 425 degrees and grease a baking sheet.

2. Lay out 1 sheet of puff pastry on the greased baking sheet.
3. Spread the Dijon mustard across the pastry sheet.
4. In a bowl, mix together the ground pork, brandy, ground cloves, black pepper, salt, and herbes de Provence.
5. Spread the pork mixture over the mustard-covered pastry.
6. Lay the second sheet of puff pastry on top and press down to seal the edges.
7. Brush with egg wash.
8. Bake for 20-25 minutes, or until golden brown.
9. Let cool and serve.

Nutrition information:
Calories: 360; Total Fat: 25g; Saturated Fat: 9g; Cholesterol: 50mg; Sodium: 162mg; Total Carbohydrate: 15g; Dietary Fiber: 1g; Sugars: 1g; Protein: 16g.

91. Boeuf en Daube

Boeuf en Daube is a classic French beef stew made using red wine, vegetables and herbs. It's the perfect comfort food and perfect for cold winter nights!
Serving: 6
Preparation Time: 10 minutes
Ready Time: 2 hours

Ingredients:
2 lb beef short ribs
1 onion, diced
2 carrots, peeled and diced
2 celery stalks, diced
1/2 cup tomato paste
1/2 cup red wine
3 cloves garlic, chopped
2 bay leaves
1 tablespoon chopped fresh thyme
1 teaspoon chopped fresh rosemary
Salt and pepper to taste

Instructions:
1. Preheat oven to 300°F.
2. In a large Dutch oven, heat oil over medium-high heat.
3. Add the beef short ribs to the pan and brown on all sides. Add the onions, carrots, celery, tomato paste, red wine, garlic, bay leaves, thyme and rosemary and season with salt and pepper to taste.
4. Cover the pot and transfer to the oven. Cook for 2 hours, stirring occasionally.
5. Serve the beef en daube hot with crusty bread or over mashed potatoes.

Nutrition information:
Calories: 262, Protein: 25g, Total Fat: 10g, Carbohydrates: 7g, Fiber: 1g, Sodium: 66mg

92. Escargots à la Bourguignonne

Escargots à la Bourguignonne is a classic French dish, made with snails baked in a garlic butter sauce. This decadent recipe is sure to wow any crowd.
Serving: 4
Preparation Time: 10 minutes
Ready Time: 40 minutes

Ingredients:
- 24 large fresh snails
- 1/2 cup butter
- 4 cloves garlic, minced
- 1/4 cup parsley, chopped
- Salt and pepper to taste
- 1/2 cup dry white wine

Instructions:
1. Rinse the snails and place them in a pot filled with boiling salty water. Simmer for about 10 minutes.
2. Drain the snails and place them in a baking dish.
3. Melt the butter in a small saucepan over medium-low heat and add the garlic; cook for a few minutes.

4. Pour the garlic butter over the snails and sprinkle with parsley. Add salt and pepper to taste.
5. Pour the white wine into the baking dish and bake in a preheated 350°F oven for about 30 minutes.
6. Serve the snails hot.

Nutrition information:
Calories: 189, Fat: 16 g, Cholesterol: 30 mg, Sodium: 100 mg, Carbohydrates: 3 g, Protein: 3 g

93. Tarte aux Pommes

Tarte aux Pommes is a traditional French apple tart that is easy to make and is full of apples and delicious, caramelized sugar. It is the perfect way to end any meal or enjoy as a snack.
Serving: 8
Preparation Time: 25 minutes
Ready Time: 1 hour and 15 minutes

Ingredients:
- 2 sheets of ready-rolled pastry
- 4 Granny Smith apples
- 2 tablespoons of granulated sugar
- 1 tablespoon of butter
- 2 tablespoons of apricot jam
- 2 tablespoons of water
- Icing sugar for dusting

Instructions:
1. Preheat oven to 350 F / 180 C
2. Line an 8-inch tart tin with one sheet of pastry.
2. Peel, core, and thinly slice the apples.
3. Place the slices in a bowl and sprinkle with sugar.
4. Arrange the apples slices in a circular pattern on the pastry.
5. Dot with the butter.
6. Cut the remaining pastry sheet into strips and arrange in a lattice pattern over the top of the tart.
7. Brush with the apricot jam mixed with the water.

8. Bake in preheated oven for around 45 minutes or until golden.
9. Sprinkle with icing sugar and serve.

Nutrition information: Per serving (1/8 slice) - Calories: 224, Fat: 8g, Sodium: 176mg, Carbs: 34g, Fiber: 3g, Sugars: 13g, Protein: 2g.

CONCLUSION

The Savoring 93 Classics: A Cookbook is a comprehensive, accessible, and enjoyable book for anyone looking to get started with cooking. This cookbook contains delicious recipes for classic dishes from around the world, and presents each with ease and clarity. The step-by-step instructions, the beautiful photography, and the global approach all make for a cookbook that is sure to become a favorite among home cooks.

Whether you're just starting out or a seasoned home chef, Savoring 93 Classics: A Cookbook has something to offer. From French moussaka to American clam chowder and from Spanish paella to Thai pad thai, this book has it all. The clear instructions and helpful tips make it possible for even the most inexperienced cooks to create something delicious.

Savoring 93 Classics: A Cookbook is a great resource for anyone looking to broaden their culinary horizons and to explore the world of food. It provides delicious comfort food recipes as well as delicious international dishes. This cookbook is a must have for anyone looking to cook meals that are both classic and inspired. With its clear directions and wide variety of recipes, Savoring 93 Classics: A Cookbook is sure to be a staple in any kitchen or cookbook collection.

Made in the USA
Columbia, SC
05 October 2023

24017355R00057